Python
Practice Lab

Python Practice Lab

Learn How to Code through Interactive Examples

Angelica Lim · Victor Cheung

Princeton University Press

Princeton and Oxford

Published by Princeton University Press
41 William Street, Princeton, New Jersey 08540
99 Banbury Road, Oxford OX2 6JX

press.princeton.edu

GPSR Authorized Representative: Easy Access System Europe - Mustamäe tee 50, 10621 Tallinn, Estonia, gpsr.requests@easproject.com

All Rights Reserved

ISBN (pbk.) 978-0-691-24360-3
ISBN (epub) 978-0-691-28262-6
ISBN (PDF) 978-0-691-24363-4
Library of Congress Control Number: 2025948509

British Library Cataloging-in-Publication Data is available

Editorial: Hallie Stebbins and Chloe Coy
Production Editorial: Karen Carter
Text and Cover Design: Wanda España
Production: Erin Suydam
Publicity: William Pagdatoon

Cover Credit: Danil Cetvericov / Alamy Stock Vector

This book has been composed in Times New Roman and Halyard Display

Printed in the United States of America

10 9 8 7 6 5 4 3 2 1

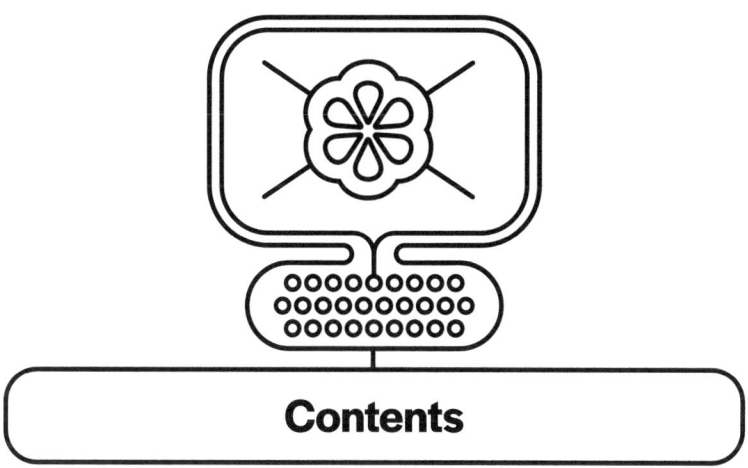

Contents

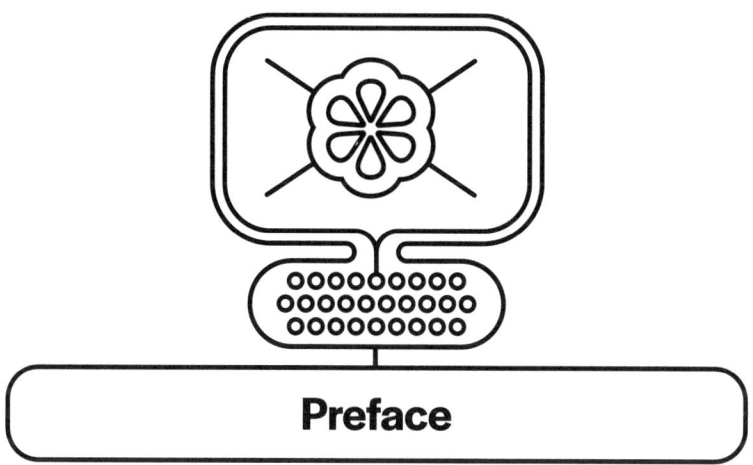

Preface

Interactive chatbots are taking the world by storm! Are you interested in creating interactive programs but don't know where to start? Do you have no coding background and want a fun introduction to computer science (CS)? Or, perhaps you are a teacher looking for a structured program to cover the areas in CS, while keeping examples interesting and fresh for your students?

In this book, you will learn basic programming by writing Python programs that mimic interactive chatbots. While this introductory book is *not* about how to code an advanced artificial intelligence, you will gain skills necessary for basic coding while learning about artificial intelligence concepts such as recommendation systems, computer vision, and big data.

The curriculum presented in this workbook has been taught as an introduction to CS and programming course at Simon Fraser University in British Columbia, Canada, to over a thousand students, and to both majors and nonmajors in Computing Science. The course is designed to teach through real-life situations, and to give students the opportunity for creative thinking. Reflecting on the course, a student shared:

> Although I have been interested in programming since high school, I was always too intimidated to try it. I am really glad to have finally taken this course because I found that I enjoyed programming and problem solving more than I expected to. I had so much fun throughout the entire semester, and will be taking more computing science courses this summer—hopefully I can pursue a minor!

We hope this book will inspire the same enthusiasm in you to pursue a deeper understanding and appreciation of CS!

WHAT ARE CHATBOTS?

In this book, we use the term "chatbots" to describe interactive programs that use text as input and output. In particular, these programs converse with the user and have a text-based interface, similar to that of a messaging app. You will be developing these interactive programs, which your friends and you can try!

HOW IS THIS BOOK DIFFERENT?

This workbook is meant to be engaging, hands-on, and example-driven to help you become a confident coder. In line with our theme, interactive chatbots, natural language and text strings are used early on as the main building blocks for learning about program structures, rather than math. This approach demonstrates the use of CS in many diverse areas and fields. Additionally, code comprehension exercises, traditionally containing terse, single-letter variables, are rewritten in equivalent code with inclusive and approachable variable names. In each chapter, the reader is challenged to write a full program based on the topics and the provided examples. Finally, a selection of projects is presented at the end of the book, to integrate the concepts learned through all the chapters.

By the end of this book, you will become well-versed in traditional introductory algorithms and become fluent in programming in Python 3. The learning outcomes for this toolkit are roughly equivalent to those of *How to Think Like a Computer Scientist* (Ch. 1–12, 15) (https://runestone.academy/ns/books/published/thinkcspy/index.html).

IS THIS BOOK RIGHT FOR ME?

The audience for this workbook includes:

- anyone who wants to learn how to program by coding fun, working programs that gradually become more complex;
- instructors teaching Python to beginners who need motivating examples and exercises for their classes; and
- students wishing to have a reference to examples taught by their instructors and wishing to build complete and functional programs.

WHAT IS THIS BOOK NOT?

This book is not a stand-alone CS textbook. It is a hands-on workbook that provides basic coverage of all the necessary concepts needed for introductory CS through examples and exercises, without overburdening the reader with details behind individual topics (e.g., how are variables represented in memory? what are modules?). Additional explanations and exercises to practice specific skills are linked to from this workbook as additional resources from this workbook.

ROADMAP

Here is a short guide to the contents of this book. Chapters 1 to 4.2 focus on learning the basics of programming in Python 3, while Chapters 4.3 to 6 introduce classic algorithms and hands-on projects to deepen your knowledge of CS.

Chapter 1, "Getting Started," explains the concept of an algorithm and gets you up and running with your first, "Hello, World," program.

Chapter 2, "Chatbots," introduces a broad range of concepts by progressively building more and more advanced programs that we call "bots." Chapter 2.1 focuses on the string data type and the many things you can do with it: assign it to a variable, concatenate it, compare it with other strings in conditionals (`if`/`else`), assign user input to it, create a list of them, and even choose one randomly from a list. Chapter 2.2 introduces the `for`-loop and integers, while building upon previous knowledge, such as that of string methods and nested conditionals.

Chapter 3, "Recommendation Systems," continues to build upon Chapter 2, expanding more on data types, manipulation of numbers (including floating-point numbers), division operators, accumulators, and lists using indexing. It also ventures deeper into loops by introducing nested loops and using them to access files. Finally, this chapter introduces dictionaries.

Chapter 4, "Graphics and Computer Vision," introduces the `while`-loop, expanding your understanding of functions through defining your own functions and modules. This chapter explains 2D arrays and color representation using RGB images. A simple Python course could end here, but we end the chapter with an introduction to recursion, an important concept in the field of CS.

Chapter 5, "Internet and Big Data," assumes that you now have the basics of Python programming under your belt. It provides a basic introduction to classic CS algorithms of sorting and searching, and to modern list processing algorithms such as map, filter and reduce.

Finally, Chapter 6, "Expert Projects," provides some sample applications you can build with the knowledge you've gained from this book.

DEEPEN YOUR UNDERSTANDING

Your learning doesn't stop here! Deepen your understanding of the topics by reviewing and trying activities linked from our companion website https://press.princeton.edu/books/paperback/9780691243603/python-practice-lab. The activities are also listed here for your reference:

Chapter 1 (from *How to Think Like a Computer Scientist*):

- Chapter 1: General Introduction

Chapter 2.1 (from *How to Think Like a Computer Scientist*):

- Chapter 2: Simple Python Data
- Chapter 5: Python Modules
- Chapter 7: Selection
- Chapter 9.3: Operations on Strings
- Chapter 10.2: List Values

Chapter 2.2 (from *How to Think Like a Computer Scientist*):

- Chapters 1.7 to 1.9: Different Types of Errors
- Chapter 9.5 - String Methods
- Chapter 9.13 - The `in` and `not` in Operators
- Chapter 10.5 - List Membership
- Chapters 4.4 and 4.5 – The `for`-Loop

Chapter 3.1 (from *How to Think Like a Computer Scientist*):

- Chapter 2 - Simple Python Data (Review)
- Chapters 4.4 to 4.7 - `for`-Loop and `for`-Loop with `range` Function (except `turtle` Examples)

- Chapter 6.5.1 - The Accumulation Pattern
- Chapter 9.5 - String Methods
- Chapter 9.13 - The in and not in Operators
- Chapters 10.3 to 10.5 - List Length to List Membership
- Chapter 10.18 - Accumulator Pattern

Chapter 3.2 (from *How to Think Like a Computer Scientist*):

- Chapters 10.1 to 10.8 - Lists
- Chapters 11.1 to 11.6 - Files

Chapter 4.1 (from *How to Think Like a Computer Scientist*):

- Chapters 4.1 to 4.3 and Chapter 4.6 to 4.9 - Python Turtle and the Range Function
- Chapters 6.1, 6.4 and 6.11 - Files

Chapter 4.2 (from *How to Think Like a Computer Scientist*):

- Chapters 6.2, 6.5, 6.6 and 6.7 - Files
- Chapters 8.3 to 8.8 and 8.11 - 2D Iteration: Image Processing. Note: This online reference on image processing is helpful for theory, but is slightly different from what we use in this book (provided as the csimage module).

Chapter 4.3 (from *How to Think Like a Computer Scientist*):

- Chapter 6.1 - What Is Recursion?
- Chapter 6.3 - Three Laws of Recursion
- Chapter 6.5 - Visualizing Recursion
- Chapter 6.6 - Sierpinski Triangle

Chapter 5.1 (from *Problem Solving with Algorithms and Data Structures Using Python*):

- Chapter 6.2 - Searching
- Chapter 6.3 - Linear Search
- Chapter 6.4 - Binary Search

Chapter 5.2 (from *Problem Solving with Algorithms and Data Structures using Python*):

- Chapter 6.6 - Sorting
- Chapter 6.8 - Selection Sort
- Chapter 6.11 - Merge Sort

Chapter 5.3 (from MIT's Software Construction course (focus on the Python notes and disregard the lambda examples):

- Map
- Functions as Values
- Filter
- Reduce

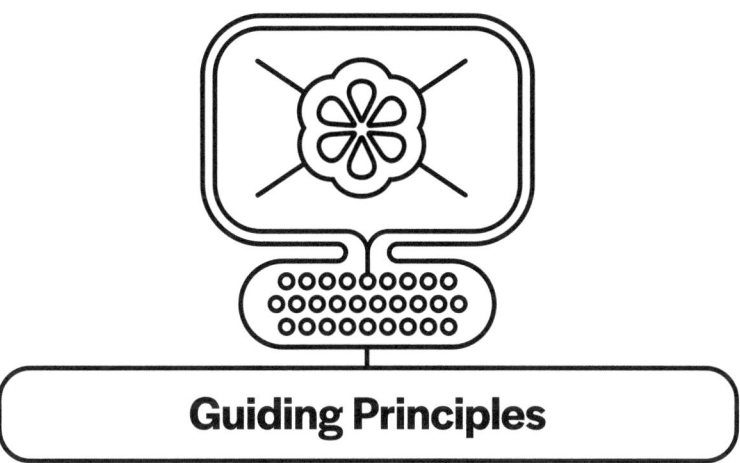

Guiding Principles

This book is a little different from those that employ traditional methods for learning computer science (CS). It uses the following philosophy to teach CS and programming.

- **Make parallels with foreign language learning.** We acknowledge that CS can feel difficult at first because learning any new language, like Chinese or French, takes time and practice. But once you become fluent, you can translate from English in your head, and communicate with a new friend—the computer!
- **Write useful code from day 1.** Our approach takes concepts and explores them in useful, end-to-end programs in each lesson. You don't have to know everything to write a program—we'll start from simple ones that you can write from day 1 and build on that to create more sophisticated ones.
- **Introduce one or two concepts at a time, in context.** Sample programs are carefully crafted so that you are not overloaded with multiple concepts at a time. And just as when learning a natural language, new concepts are introduced embedded in real programs and situations, not in isolation.
- **Design algorithms in English.** Thinking of a solution and putting it into code are two different processes, especially at first. We suggest that you design the algorithm flow in English first, then translate it into Python.
- **Handle strings first.** We reduce cognitive overload by exploring strings (sequences of characters that form words and sentences), and all their possibilities (conditionals, loops, etc.), first. This allows you to write useful and practical programs early, adding the complexity of multiple data types later.
- **Construct with creativity.** Exercises are open-ended rather than looking for a right answer. We reinforce from the beginning the idea that programming is a creative endeavor.
- **Share code with others.** We make it a delight to build programs and share them with friends and family. We use an online coding space like online-python.com or trinket.io so that you can take pride in your work and have others try it out!
- **Focus on fluency.** Our ultimate goal is to help you become a fluent coder. We deliver practice questions that ask you to write full programs from scratch.

- **Write beautiful, understandable code.** Obscure, tricky code is often used for tests of understanding, but we emphasize that real code written by professionals is highly readable, and uses descriptive variable names. No longer are variables limited to i, j, and k!
- **Showcase fields in CS.** You will learn coding through exploration units in contemporary fields in CS, such as computer vision, natural language processing, and recommendation systems.

HOW TO USE THIS BOOK

This workbook is designed to be used as an example-driven book to guide your learning of concepts in CS and Python programming. Each chapter unit begins with a scenario and a sample interactive program, followed by a list of relevant topics necessary to implement the program. As the chapter progresses, details and an explanation of each topic are provided. At the end of each chapter, additional practice exercises are included to reinforce these topics.

We recommend using this workbook in a way that depends on who you are.

IF YOU ARE A SELF-DIRECTED LEARNER OR STUDENT...

If you have never coded before and want to use this book as a guide for your learning, you have come to the right place! Read through each chapter and program listing, and try to run the example programs in your Python interpreter. Retyping the code from this book will help you learn and practice, so don't skip this step! You'll also be able to run the interactive programs and modify them, which we'll sometimes ask you to do. Next, after each subsection, check the list of external resources in Preface—Deepen Your Understanding, which links to online resources and practice questions to solidify your learning. Finally, test your mastery of the topics by completing the practice coding exercises, which each results in creating a small chatbot. Focus on writing the requested programs from scratch, then share them with your family and friends to test and play with!

IF YOU ARE AN INSTRUCTOR...

Use the scenarios as motivating examples to intrigue your students and drive the topics. Download the slides and code from our companion website (and feel free to tailor them to your class), and use in-class time to challenge your students with the practice exercises. Point your students to the additional readings for further explanations and practice exercises related to each chapter.

Python
Practice Lab

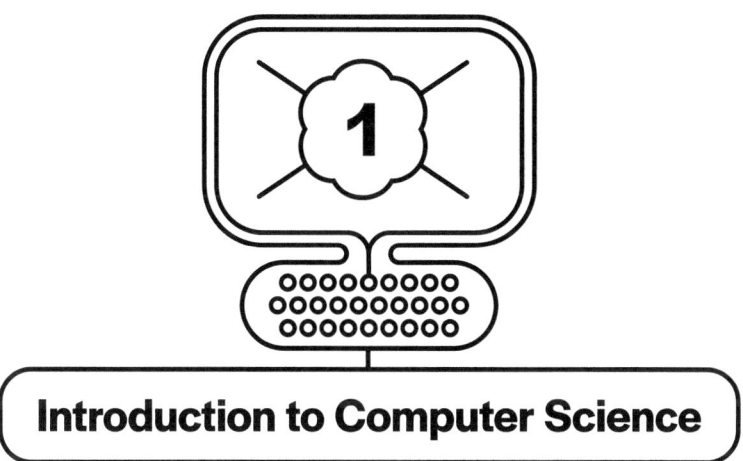

Introduction to Computer Science

Congratulations on taking your first step into CS!

In this first unit, you'll learn what computer science (CS) is and where it came from, and start to learn about how it works. You'll get set up with the tools that we'll be using in the following chapters to help you become a proficient computer scientist by the end of the book.

CS topics in this chapter:

- Algorithms
- Comments
- Output

1.1   WELCOME TO CS!

CS IS PROBLEM SOLVING

If you like solving problems, you have come to the right place! In CS, we solve problems by designing and developing two components:

- **Algorithms**, which are a way of thinking
- **Code**, which is a way of communicating

In this book, we will be designing our algorithms in English, and translating them into the Python programming language. This will allow us to communicate with computers to solve our problems.

WHAT ARE ALGORITHMS?

An algorithm is simply a list of steps to follow in order to complete a task. For example, cookie recipes are algorithms. They have ingredients as input, and a list of steps to produce a very tasty output: cookies! Another example is IKEA furniture instructions. If you can write clear, step-by-step instructions (e.g., how to build a chair), you've got great potential as a computer scientist!

Algorithms can also be **optimized** for different things. You may want to design instructions for how to do the task as fast as possible, or in a simple way, or to minimize the space needed. For instance, in our cookie recipe example, some recipe titles might be "Chocolate chip cookies in 15 minutes" (fast) or "Easy chocolate chip cookies" (simple) or "One-bowl chocolate chip cookies" (minimizing space), optimizing for different needs. There are often multiple recipes, or algorithms, to achieve a similar result.

WHAT ARE PROGRAMMING LANGUAGES?

The computer is our fast, number crunching tool to solve problems for us. In order to communicate with the computer, we need to speak a language it understands. Programming languages have been developed to be a common language that both humans and the computer can interpret and understand.

Python, Java, and C++ are names of some programming languages. Just like English, Japanese, French, and other natural languages, they are used to communicate meaning, and each has different grammar, syntax, and vocabulary.

We say that some programming languages, such as Python and JavaScript, are **interpreted** languages, while C, C++, and Java are **compiled** languages. What does compiled mean? When you run a program, your instructions to the computer are translated from the human-readable language such as Python or C++ into 0s and 1s, which are digital signals that the computer can understand.

Translation can in happen two ways: line-by-line or in a batch. To understand this better, imagine being at the United Nations. There are professional translators who sit next to each diplomat and translate everything being said in real time. These translators are called **interpreters**. At the same meeting, there may be thick piles of documents on each desk that have been **compiled** into big translated reports before the meeting.

In the same way, Python is an **interpreted** language because the Python interpreter on your computer translates each line of code into machine code in real time, on the fly, as the program runs on your computer. With C++, the entire program is completely **compiled** into machine code before anything runs.

> Now that you know the difference between interpreted and compiled programming languages, can you list two examples of programming languages for each type?

WHAT IS PROGRAMMING?

Once we have a general algorithm design in mind, and have selected a programming language, we can begin to program! Programming itself is the process where you break a large, complex task down into smaller subtasks and constructs that are recognizable to a computer.

Common programming constructs include:

- Input
- Output
- Conditions
- Repetition
- Math or logic

We will explore all of these in the coming chapters!

DID YOU KNOW ? The first programmer was an English mathematician named Lady Ada Lovelace. In 1842, she wrote the first computer program for Charles Babbage's Analytical Engine (1837). Her first program calculated Bernoulli numbers, but she also envisioned a future where the numbers she worked with could represent more than numbers. She believed that any data represented by numbers could be processed by a machine like the Analytical Engine, to compose music, create images, or do science. Today, with our modern computers, we know that she was right!

1.1.1 Learning Outcomes

At the end of this unit, you will be able to …

- write Python comments
- explain what pseudocode is
- describe the main characteristics of an algorithm
- give an example of problem solving by subdividing tasks in to subtasks
- write a program header block (i.e., initial comments with information about the author, date, and purpose of the code)
- output `Hello World` using `print()`

1.1.2 Alien Explanations

Do you like science fiction? In this section, we'll deepen our understanding of algorithms by inventing an example that may seem strange, even alien, at first. All will be clear, soon!

Imagine that one day the Earth is visited by aliens from another planet. You have been chosen to communicate with the alien, which knows nothing about the human race. You meet the alien, which comically looks exactly like a pea-green octopus with a space helmet. Luckily, the alien happens to speak English. The first thing it says is, "I would like to learn about the human species. Please, tell me something about your daily life as a human."

You reply, "Well, we do this thing every day. We brush our teeth!"

The alien replies, "Please, human, explain 'brush our teeth.'"

EXERCISE

Explain to the alien the procedure to "brush one's teeth." You can either explain to another person nearby who takes the role of the alien (be as curious as possible!), or write out the explanation.

DEBRIEF

First off, it's not easy to explain something that comes so simply to us! You may have included the tools or input involved: a hand, a toothbrush … what else? Toothpaste? Mouth? Many components are involved. For an alien that does not have teeth or even hands, this requires patience and explanation in detail.

Secondly, what did your explanation look like? Was it a list of numbered steps? How detailed was it? Did you include aspects such as how long the brushing should last, or how much toothpaste you need? The clearer your steps were, the closer to algorithmic thinking they will be.

Spoiler alert: Your computer is just like this alien! It has no idea about the human world. We therefore need to be patient with it and explain our algorithms very clearly. Luckily, to communicate with our computer, we have the common language of Python, which we will learn in this book. Once we learn how to communicate clearly in Python, we can ask our computer to do what we want!

1.1.3   Writing and Running Your Programs

Throughout this book you'll see a lot of the following:

```
1   print("Hello World!")
```

These are code samples that you can copy and paste to a Python interpreter to try them out yourself or experiment with by making changes to it (the number on the left is the line number; you do not have to write it in your code). There are two main kinds of coding environments with Python interpreters you can use.

ONLINE CODING ENVIRONMENTS

Online coding environments are websites that provide a workspace for you to write and run your programs in an Internet browser window. Depending on the service provider, some offer saving your code under a user account and/or directly to your computer. Some also offer subscription plans with more features. Here are a few that we find quite useful and that are available on some of the most common operating systems (i.e., Windows, macOS, Linux).

Online Python (https://www.online-python.com) is an in-browser Integrated Development Environment (IDE) for Python. You can download your work as a `.py` or `.zip` file and can upload text files, too. You do not have to create an account to use its services, but it has some limitations, such as not being able to upload images. One great feature is that once you create a program, you can share a link to it with your friends and family. Online Python is a simple but good IDE to use.

Trinket (https://trinket.io) is another in-browser IDE that lets you write, run, and share your programs on its online platform. It also includes some lessons for users to learn about coding and provides some other ways to program (via Blocks). It has fewer features than the offline coding environments described below but still works well. You have to sign up for a free account with some limitations to use its services.

Programiz (https://www.programiz.com/) is a learning platform offering free and paid courses for various programming languages, including Python. Similarly to Trinket, it includes a free online compiler and lets you write, run, and share your code without signing up. Besides programming languages, it also offers courses on data structures and algorithms, which are important next steps if you are interested in CS.

OFFLINE CODING ENVIRONMENTS

One obvious shortcoming of the online coding environments is that you have to stay connected to the Internet to use them. If you want to write and run your programs on your computer without worrying about access to the Internet, installing an offline application is the way to go. Note that we use Python 3 in this book.

Python IDLE (https://www.python.org/downloads) is from the official creator of the Python language. It is simple but has all the things you need to develop your programs in Python. When you download and install a Python version, it will install both the interpreter and an application called IDLE (Integrated Development and Learning Environment). Once installed, you can start IDLE and use the top menu to write and run your programs.

Mu (https://codewith.mu) is a Python IDE created for beginner programmers. It includes a few useful modules (e.g., pygame) that other IDEs might have to install separately, so one can start quickly without worrying about downloading extra modules. The idea is to minimize setup and downloads so that beginners can start as soon as they install the application. The application also has a few useful features for beginners to customize their editor and check their code.

PyCharm (https://www.jetbrains.com/pycharm) is a fully-fledged IDE for Python development. It has many development tools such as on-the-fly code analysis, a graphical debugger, a unit tester, and version control (it's completely okay if you don't know what these are), which are great for projects of bigger scale but might be excessive for beginners. There are two versions for download: a paid Professional version with other language support, and a free Community version, which is more than sufficient in most cases.

SUMMARY

There are also other coding environments and tools out there that we haven't covered, and those that we have covered may change over time. So it is up to you to decide which one you want to use. However, no matter which coding environment and tools you choose to use, the idea is the same: plan your algorithm, write the code for it, run it, and keep improving it—that's the way to learn how to code.

1.1.4   Motivational Quote Generator

Hooray! You have made it to the first programming example in this book! In many books, the first programming example you'll see is the "Hello World" program. But let's do something different here.

> "Hello World!" is an in-joke within computer scientists and programmers because this is typically the very first program they write when they learn a programming language. A Hello World program illustrates the basic syntax of the language by properly displaying a simple greeting message.

We all need a few words of wisdom or encouragement from time to time—this is why people like opening fortune cookies and putting up posters with motivational phrases. In this section, let's write a Motivational Quote Generator program that says something motivating, wise, or funny, if you like, to the user.

WHO IS THE USER? Programmers build applications for people to use it. The people who use your application are called users.

```
1  # Motivational Quote Generator
2  # Author:
3  # Date:
4
5  print("If you can dream it, you can do it.")
```

In the code sample above, let's identify several important parts of a program:

- Lines 1–3 are **comments** that are not interpreted or run by the computer. Instead, their purpose is to provide useful information about the code to the person reading or writing the code. In Python, each line of comment begins with the # symbol. In this book, we call the comments at the top of your file (typically containing information such as title, author, and date) the **header**.
- Line 4 is an empty line, which will be ignored by the computer. It is there to visually partition the code so that the code is easier for humans to read. You can have as many empty lines as you want, but it's best to use them with a purpose, and consistently.
- Line 5 is the code executed by the computer. It represents a single command: **print** a sentence to the screen. Try replacing the sentence in the sample code with other words (or even a combination of strings and numbers separated by commas). The sentence must be surrounded by quotation marks. If you want to print the quotation mark itself, you must precede it with a backslash, like this: print("As they say, \" Practice makes perfect!\"").

Comments are important parts of the code. In addition to the header, we use comments to explain the code, leave notes, and provide documentation. If you want to have more than one line of comments, you can use **multiline docstrings** by surrounding the lines with three double quotes: """.

1.1.5   Review Questions

Time to test how much you understand the content in this chapter! If you need to, feel free to go back and review.

THEORY AND UNDERSTANDING

- What are the two components of CS we'll study in this workbook?
- What is an example of an algorithm?
- What is the name of the programming language we'll use in this book? Is it interpreted or compiled?
- Where can we practice coding online? Offline?
- What goes into the header of a program?
- What does learning a programming language have in common with learning a natural language?

SYNTAX SELF-CHECK

What do the following functions and keywords mean?

- `print("Hello, World")`
- `print("I have", 1)`
- `#`
- `"a string"`
- `"""`
  ```
  a multiline string
  another line
  """
  ```

1.1.6 Practice Exercises

CODING

Now it's time for you to practice by writing some code. When you are finished, you can go to the Solutions section on our companion website to compare your answers with ours. Note that there can be many answers to the same question, so don't worry if your code is not exactly the same as ours. For now, the important thing is that your code produce the results you expect.

DISPLAYING A SENTENCE

Write a line of code that outputs the following sentence to the screen:

```
Dr. Evil: Back in the 60's, we developed a sophisticated heat beam we called a "laser".
```

MOTIVATIONAL QUOTE GENERATOR

Write your own Python program displaying a motivation quote. Begin with a header that matches your desired title, your name, and the date. Then replace the quote with one of your choices based on the sample code we showed you earlier. Use the Run button to make sure it prints on the screen as expected.

1.1.7 Glossary

- **code (aka source code)**, the vocabulary used when writing a computer program. There are different kinds/levels of code, including pseudocode, which is easily readable by humans, programming code, which follows the rules of a specific language, and machine code, which is understood by the computer but typically not by a human.
- **pseudocode**, code that is written in plain language so that it can be read by humans. Pseudocode typically follows some structural conventions, such as line breaks and indentations, to indicate order of execution. It uses some standard keywords, such as `repeat` and `if-then`, and symbols, such as + and := , to represent programming logic, but omits language-specific details such as variable declarations. Many algorithms are written in this form for computer scientists to quickly communicate their ideas without fixating on a particular programming language.
- **programming**, the process of (a) breaking a large, complex task into smaller and smaller tasks until they are simple enough to be performed with sequences of basic constructs, including input/output, repetition, conditionals and logic and (b) writing them using code.

- **algorithm**, a step-by-step list of instructions to complete a task or solve a problem. There are usually many different ways to complete the same task or solve the same problem, and the clearer each step is, the better (there are different ways to make an algorithm better, e.g., faster, or requiring less space).
- **header**, a block of comments providing some information about the program preceding the code. It includes the name(s) of the author(s), the creation and modification dates, and a high-level description of the program.
- **comment**, a special section adjacent to the code and written in plain English explaining what that code does. It is for human readers to understand the code and is indicated by a special symbol (# in Python) so the computer will ignore it when executing the code. It can be a single sentence or a short paragraph.
- **interpretation**, the process used by the computer to execute the source code. For an interpreted programming language, the source code is translated directly into machine code during execution. Python and JavaScript are examples of this.
- **compilation**, the other process used by the computer to execute the source code, where the source code is first translated into machine/object (aka compiled) code and then executed. C/C++ and Java are examples of compiled programming languages.

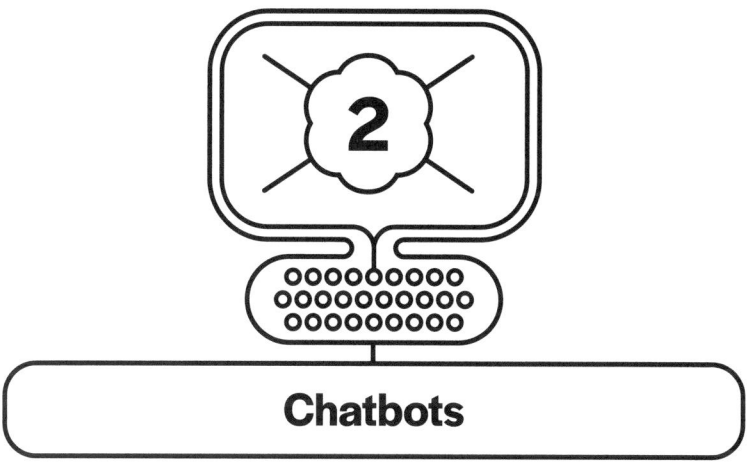

Chatbots

Many modern computer applications enable some form of interaction, or even conversation, between the computer and the user. Here you'll learn how to create interactive chatbot applications in Python.

In this unit, you'll learn about the basics of programming through exercises loosely based on interactive chatbots like Amazon's Alexa or Apple's Siri. The chatbot programs that you'll be writing include:

- Greetings Chatbot
- Horoscope Bot
- Fortune Cookie Generator
- Food Bot
- Mindreader Game
- New Year's Bot
- Star Wars Bot

ChatGPT and other recent "large language model" chatbots are powered by neural networks trained on vast amounts of data, and are not necessarily programmed by hand in the manner you will learn to do so here. But, early chatbots were programmed in a similar way to that you will explore in this chapter, and Python is the de facto programming language in artificial intelligence development. By writing these chatbot programs in Python, you'll learn about outputting to the screen, creating lists, working with text, and changing output depending on conditions.

CS topics in this unit:

- Variables
- Concatenation
- Input
- Lists
- The random module
- Conditionals
- Boolean statements and expressions
- Error types
- Robustness of a program

- String methods
- The in keyword
- Chaining functions
- for-loops
- Lists from input

2.1   CHATBOTS WITH PERSONALITY

In this unit, you will be learning how to build basic interactive chatbots that you can communicate with! Here is an example:

```
What year are we in?
2026
How old are you currently?
21
You will be 44 years old in 2049!
```

You can also try the sample code yourself:

```
1  # Your age in 2049 bot
2  # Author:
3  # Date:
4  # Description: This bot will ask you
5  # what year it is in and how old you
6  # currently are, then it'll tell you
7  # your age in 2049
8
9  # Ask user what year it is in
10 print("What year are we in?")
11
12 # Get the user's reply
13 currentYear = input()
14
15 # Ask user what age they currently are
16 print("How old are you currently?")
17
18 # Get the user's reply
19 userAge = input()
20
21 # Calculate how old the user will be in 2049
22 yearsAhead = 2049 - int(currentYear)
23 userFutureAge = int(userAge) + yearsAhead
24
25 # Tell the user how old they will be in 2049
26 print("You will be", userFutureAge, "years old in 2049!")
```

A few interesting things happen when you run this program:

- It asks the user two questions and captures the answers
- It converts the user inputs into values that can be used for calculation
- It performs some calculations and prints the result

As you might notice, when the user provides different answers, the program will print different results. Now, is it possible for the program to say something appropriate depending on the user's age in 2049? The answer is yes, and you'll find out how in this unit.

2.1.1   Learning Outcomes

At the end of this unit, you will be able to ...

DESIGN AND PLAN PROGRAMS

- design/plan an algorithm, e.g., using comments or pseudocode
- apply some common problem solving strategies, such as breaking down the problem into smaller pieces

CONSOLE INPUT AND OUTPUT

- obtain input in Python from the terminal to a variable
- receive input from the terminal without saving it to a variable

VARIABLES AND DATATYPES

- assign a value to a variable using =
- articulate the constraints and conventions on variable naming
- give examples of different types of data, although string is the focus for now

STRING AND LIST BASICS

- identify the string data type, " "
- output a string variable in a print statement
- concatenate two strings with +
- create a list of strings and assign it to a variable, using [ ]

CONDITIONAL STATEMENTS

- use if and elif statements with ==
- use the **else** clause

BOOLEAN EXPRESSIONS, LOGICAL AND RELATIONAL OPERATORS

- use logical operators **and, or** and **not**
- use comparison operators such as <, > and == in a conditional statement
- analyze a Boolean expression in terms of what it can be evaluated to (**True/False**)
- combine Boolean expressions, e.g., **x or y**, using strings only (for now)
- print a Boolean expression

IMPORTING A MODULE

- use the **random.choice()** function on a list (including **import random**)
- explain what the . after a module name does
- understand that modules contain functions
- consistently place import statements at the top of the program, after the header

2.1.2   Greetings Chatbot

Let's begin by creating a Greetings chatbot. What do you think a chatbot should say when it starts a conversation? Perhaps it might say hi or some sort of greeting phrase. It might also be nice to personalize it by having it say the user's name. This means that the program needs to be able to read text typed by the user (e.g., name) and store it somewhere within the program.

Open up your Python file, and type out the following. First, begin by writing the header, with a title, your name, and the date. Then, design your program by writing out the algorithm steps using comments.

```
1  # Greetings Chatbot
2  # Author:
3  # Date:
4
5  # Say hi, what's your name?
6  # Get the user's name
7  # Respond nice to meet you, <name>
```

Now that we've designed the general flow of our chatbot, let's see how we can translate our algorithm, line by line, into Python. The first comment should be straightforward to translate into Python. Think about the Motivational Quote Generator you wrote in the last chapter!

```
1  # Greetings Chatbot
2  # Author:
3  # Date:
4
5  # Say hi, what's your name?
6  print("Hi, what's your name?")
7
8  # Get the user's name
9  # Respond nice to meet you, <name>
```

Next, we'll learn the code for obtaining input text from the user, and storing that text into a variable. As you can see, you can use the input() function that will allow the user to type some text into the program. We create a variable called user and use = to store the inputted name into it.

```
1  # Greetings Chatbot
2  # Author:
3  # Date:
4
5  # Say hi, what's your name?
6  print("Hi, what's your name?")
7
8  # Get the user's name
```

```
 9   user = input()
10
11   # Respond nice to meet you, <name>
```

> Both print() and input() are Python elements called **functions**. For now, you can consider them as bits of code that you can use to add functionality into your program. We will dive more into what functions are in Chapter 4.

Finally, we can take the user's name and repeat it back to them. To do this, we take the string Nice to meet you and use + to tack on the contents of the variable user. This gluing together is called **concatenation**. Notice that we also have to remember to write a comma and space beforehand.

```
 1   # Greetings Chatbot
 2   # Author:
 3   # Date:
 4
 5   # Say hi, what's your name?
 6   print("Hi, what's your name?")
 7
 8   # Get the user's name
 9   user = input()
10
11   # Respond nice to meet you, <name>
12   print("Nice to meet you, " + user)
```

> We say that "Hi, what's your name?" is a **string** data type. "Nice to meet you," is also a string (the quotation marks are included in the code to indicate that the characters between them form a string; the marks themselves are not part of the string). Finally, the input() function also returns a **string** with the characters that the user typed, and therefore the variable user contains a string as well!

You have created your first interactive chatbot! Give it a try by running the entire program and typing with your chatbot. Try also inputting different names.

You will notice that the program responds with the name of the user and changes when the user inputs a different name. What happens here is that at line 9 the program does two things: (1) it waits for the user to input their name, and then (2) it stores the user input (their name) in a variable with name user. Later, in line 12, it is able to recall the user input using the same variable. This is handy because if the program wants to recall the user input again later in the program, it can simply refer to the variable again by its name.

Now, let's continue the conversation. We'll start by designing our conversation flow, again with comments first. Let's ask the user about their favourite book and make a comment.

```
 1  # Greetings Chatbot
 2  # Author:
 3  # Date:
 4
 5  # Say hi, what's your name?
 6  print("Hi, what's your name?")
 7
 8  # Get the user's name
 9  user = input()
10
11  # Respond nice to meet you, <name>
12  print("Nice to meet you, " + user)
13
14  # Ask what your favourite book is
15  # Let the user respond
16  # Make a comment about it
```

Can you now try to complete the program in Python, based on the example we've seen earlier?

How did you do? There are many ways you could have completed the program. Perhaps you asked for the name of the book, and repeated back the book's name. Another way you could have completed the program was to *not* store the input from the user in a variable. Here is an example.

```
 1  # Greetings Chatbot
 2  # Author:
 3  # Date:
 4
 5  # Say hi, what's your name?
 6  print("Hi, what's your name?")
 7
 8  # Get the user's name
 9  user = input()
10
11  # Respond nice to meet you, <name>
12  print("Nice to meet you, " + user)
13
14  # Ask what your favourite book is
15  print("What is your favourite book?")
16
17  # Let the user respond
18  input()
19
20  # Make a comment about it
21  print("Oh nice!")
```

Note that in line 18 in the code above, we didn't store the response from the user in a variable. That's because we decided to make a generic response, and didn't need to use the response in line 21. This is another way you could have completed the program. In any case, we hope you enjoyed creating your first interactive chatbot! If you used any of the online programming environments, send a link to your chatbot to a friend to let them try it!

> Here we introduce a fundamental CS topic: **variables**. As illustrated in the program example, it is simply something that the program uses to store pieces of information that it can recall and use later. The name of the variable is used to uniquely identify a piece of information (challenge: there are some rules about what is a valid variable name; investigate what they are!). They are called variables because the program can also change the information stored in them; thus their content *varies*.

Before moving on to the next section, let's try one last thing: remove line 6 and move the greeting sentence "Hi, what's your name?" directly into the parentheses of the line 9 input function like this:

```
user = input("Hi, what's your name?")
```

This combines lines 6 and 9 into one line, and allows the user to type their answer to the right of the question, rather than below. This is an alternative way to use input(), but for interactive chatbots, we suggest the first way, which we showed you earlier, to simulate a back-and-forth conversation on separate lines, similarly to chat or messaging applications.

INTRODUCING LISTS

Now we have a chatbot that can greet the user by their name, ask about their book preference, and provide a response! But as you run the program a few more times, you'll notice the response is always the same; it gets a bit repetitive. How can we make the interaction more life-like and exciting?

Let's consider the following approach, where we create a few possible responses and randomly choose one of them.

```
1   # Greetings Chatbot
2   # Author:
3   # Date:
4
5   import random
6
7   # Say hi, what's your name?
8   print("Hi, what's your name?")
9
10  # Get the person's name
11  user = input()
12
13  # Respond nice to meet you, <name>
14  print("Nice to meet you, " + user)
15
16  # Ask what your favourite book is
17  print("What is your favourite book?")
```

```
18
19  # Let the user respond
20  input()
21
22  # Make a not-too-repetitive response in 3 steps:
23  # Create a list of possible response
24  # Choose one randomly from the list
25  # Say that random response
```

For instance, we can think of a few responses the chatbot can provide, such as, "Oh, nice!" and "That's a good one." To allow the program to use one of these responses, we need a way to store them. We'll now introduce a programming construct called a **list** that allows us to store a sequence of values in a single variable. We call this data type a list because the order in which the values are stored will remain the same, as when you list items on a piece of paper. This will become handy later when we want to specify a particular item in the list, or access all the items one by one.

To create a list in Python, we use a pair of square brackets, [and], and put all the values we want to store inside them (separated by commas). Sometimes the list can be quite long, making it hard to read the code if everything is in one line. We suggest breaking it into several lines, as in lines 25–27.

> Python expects each line of code to be in one line. However, to help with readability, we can use the continuation character \ at the end of each line to create multiline code. Yet, when writing the content of a list, we do not need to use the continuation character, as long as we break the lines after a comma.

```
 1  # Greetings Chatbot
 2  # Author:
 3  # Date:
 4
 5  import random
 6
 7  # Say hi, what's your name?
 8  print("Hi, what's your name?")
 9
10  # Get the person's name
11  user = input()
12
13  # Respond nice to meet you, <name>
14  print("Nice to meet you, " + user)
15
16  # Ask what your favourite book is
17  print("What is your favourite book?")
18
19  # Let the user respond
20  input()
```

```
21
22    # Make a not-too-repetitive response in 3 steps:
23
24    # Create a list of possible response
25    responses = ["Oh, nice!", "That's a good one.",
26                 "Hmm, strange taste.", "blah blah blah",
27                 "Whoa there.", "Hahahhaa!"]
28
29    # Choose one randomly from the list
30    # Say that random response
```

As you can see, we've created a list with six possible values. Specifically, this list contains six strings. Now that we have a list of possible phrases, we need to find a way to choose which phrase the program should use for the response. To make the selection random (different each time you run the program), we add an import statement (line 5) to allow us to use a function called `random.choice`, which randomly selects an item from a list it receives (line 29).

> We have imported the `random` module into our program. A module is a collection of useful functions that we can use in our program. To access the functions in the module, we use the . (dot) operator. Some functions are built-in in Python (such as `input()`), so we don't need to import anything, while some functions, such as `choice()`, need to be imported.

```
 1    # Greetings Chatbot
 2    # Author:
 3    # Date:
 4
 5    import random
 6
 7    # Say hi, what's your name?
 8    print("Hi, what's your name?")
 9
10    # Get the person's name
11    user = input()
12
13    # Respond nice to meet you, <name>
14    print("Nice to meet you, " + user)
15
16    # Ask what your favourite book is
17    print("What is your favourite book?")
18
19    # Let the user respond
20    input()
21
22    # Make a not-too-repetitive response in 3 steps:
```

```
23
24  # Make a list of possible response
25  responses = ["Oh, nice!", "That's a good one.",
26              "Hmm, strange taste.", "blah blah blah",
27              "Whoa there.", "Hahahhaa!"]
28
29  # Choose one randomly from the list
30  random_response = random.choice(responses)
31
32  # Say that random response
33  print(random_response)
```

To finish, we can see that the randomly selected item is then stored in the variable random_response (line 30) and is printed to the screen (line 33).

Run this program a few times and see the chatbot giving a random response each time!

> **TIP!** If you'd like to add some human-like pauses into your chatbot timings, add another import statement "import time" at the top of your program (just under the import random statement), and add time.sleep(1) wherever you want your program to pause for one second! Try changing 1 to other numbers, such as 1.5 or 2. Does your chatbot seem more thoughtful?

2.1.3   How's It Going Bot

The next program we will write is an interactive How's It Going chatbot. This time, our program is based on the ELIZA Rogerian psychotherapist chatbot developed at the MIT Artificial Intelligence Laboratory in 1964, which asked questions and empathized with the user.

In this program, we'll ask the user how they're feeling, and make an appropriate response. What our program needs is the ability to make decisions and execute different pieces of code depending on the situation, as determined by the user input. We call the different options "conditions."

BRANCHING USING CONDITIONAL STATEMENTS (IF/ELIF/ELSE)

Let's begin with the following algorithmic design, again written first in English comments. Sometimes, computer scientists call program sketches like these **pseudocode**, as it's not quite code, but close to it! Notice that our header also now includes a short description of the program, which can help remind you of the purpose of the program when reading it later.

```
1  # How's it going bot
2  # Author:
3  # Date:
4  # Description: This bot will ask you how it's
5  # going and make a comment depending on
```

```
 6   # how you answered
 7
 8   # Ask the user how it's going
 9   # Get the user's reply
10   # If they said Good, reply Good!
11   # Otherwise if they said Bad, reply Oh no!
```

As you can see, our program sketch contains a possible **condition**, or branching: if the user replies that they're Good, the chatbot should reply, Good! If the user says they're Bad, the chatbot replies, Oh no! You should be able to translate the first two steps of the program (lines 8 and 9) into Python, based on what you've learned so far. Give it a try!

Now, let's see how we translate our conditions into Python. We need two keywords: if, which checks our first condition (that the user typed Good), and elif (else if), which checks another condition (that the user typed Bad). Each conditional uses == to compare the reply variable's content to what the user typed, followed by a colon.

```
 1   # How's it going bot
 2   # Author:
 3   # Date:
 4   # Description: This bot will ask you how it's
 5   # going and make a comment depending on
 6   # how you answered
 7
 8   # Ask user how it's going
 9   print("How's it going?")
10
11   # Get the user's reply
12   reply = input()
13
14   # If they said Good, reply Good!
15   if reply == "Good":
16     print("Good!")
17
18   # Otherwise if they said Bad, reply Oh no!
19   elif reply == "Bad":
20     print("Oh no!")
```

You'll notice a few things about the code above. First, line 16 is **indented**. In fact, whenever the condition in line 15 is true (user typed Good), all of the indented lines immediately following it will be executed. Remember to unindent for your next case (here, the elif statement), and the rest of your program.

To indent your code, press the **tab** key on your keyboard. Python is quite flexible on what you use for indentation as long as you are consistent (e.g., two spaces, four spaces). Later, you will also have to indent your code into several levels—we'll get to that when the time comes!

Now, what if the user typed something other than Good or Bad? How could our bot be made to handle that case? We can add a default condition using the `else` keyword, as follows.

```
1   # How's it going bot
2   # Author:
3   # Date:
4   # Description: This bot will ask you how it's
5   # going and reply based on your answer
6
7   # Ask user how it's going
8   print("How's it going?")
9
10  # Get the user's reply
11  reply = input()
12
13  # If they said Good, then reply Good!
14  if reply == "Good":
15      print("Good!")
16
17  # Otherwise if they said Bad, then reply Oh no!
18  elif reply == "Bad":
19      print("Oh no!")
20
21  # Otherwise reply "I see..."
22  else:
23      print("I see...")
```

In lines 14 and 18 above, you can use the keyword **in** to check for the word anywhere in the user response. For example, line 14 becomes `if "Good" in reply`. You will learn more about this keyword later in this chapter.

THE IF/ELSE SANDWICH

As you've seen above, we have created three different potential pathways for chatbot replies. The chatbot will only choose one of these paths to execute, depending on what the user typed. This structure may be confusing at first—when do we use `if`? When do we use `elif`? Does `if` always need to come before `elif`? (Yes.) Here is a general template for creating conditional blocks like the one in our program above.

```
if condition: # The only thing required in a conditional
    # do something
elif condition2: # Optional. Can be repeated.
    # do something else
else: # Optional. Only have one else per if.
    # do something else
```

In this book, we'll informally call the construct the **if/else sandwich**. You can have as many delicious `elif` statements as you want in between your `if` and your `else`, or none at all. Also, you don't need the bottom layer of your sandwich (the `else` statement). The only thing that is necessary is the first `if` statement and the statements that will be executed in that condition. You can try stripping down your program to only the first `if` condition to check for yourself.

In the code below, you can see an example of repeated `elif` statements providing more options for our program depending on the user input.

```
1   # How's it going bot
2   # Author:
3   # Date:
4   # Description: This bot will ask you how it's
5   # going and reply based on your answer
6
7   # Ask user how it's going
8   print("How's it going?")
9
10  # Get the user's reply
11  reply = input()
12
13  # If they said Good
14  # reply Good!
15  if reply == "Good":
16    print("Good!")
17
18  # Otherwise if they said "Bad", reply "Oh no!"
19  elif reply == "Bad":
20    print("Oh no!")
21
22  # Otherwise if they're "So so", reply "Hope you feel better!"
23  elif reply == "So so":
24    print("Hope you feel better!")
25
26  # Otherwise reply "I see..."
27  else:
28    print("I see...")
```

BOOLEAN EXPRESSIONS, LOGICAL AND RELATIONAL OPERATORS

The template above puts conditions after the `if` and `elif` statements. We call these conditions Boolean expressions. But what's a Boolean expression? A Boolean expression is a piece of code that can boil down to either true or false. For example, "apples" == "apples" is True, while "apples" == "oranges" is False.

You can combine Boolean expressions with others, using, for instance, the keyword or. This will be helpful, for example, if we want to make our bot reply Good! no matter whether the user types Good, good, or great.

```
 1  # How's it going bot
 2  # Author:
 3  # Date:
 4  # Description: This bot will ask you how it's
 5  #going and reply based on your answer
 6
 7  # Ask user how it's going
 8  print("How's it going?")
 9
10  # Get the user's reply
11  reply = input()
12
13  # If they said Good,
14  # reply Good!
15  if reply == "Good" or reply == "good" or reply == "great":
16      print("Good!")
17
18  # Otherwise if they said Bad, reply Oh no!
19  elif reply == "Bad":
20      print("Oh no!")
21
22  # Otherwise reply "I see..."
23  else:
24      print("I see...")
```

The **==** in our code is an example of a **relational operator**. It compares the values on its two sides and indicates whether they have the same value (i.e., they match). It can compare numbers as well as words, and the comparison for words is strict and case-sensitive: if the capitalization is different, the values will be considered different! Thus we need to compare to both Good and good, for example. Some other relational operators, which we'll look at later in the book, are <, > and >=, etc.

Try to add a few possible cases in line 19 so that instead of Bad, if the user types bad or poor, our bot will still reply Oh no! The code is getting longer, but as you test your program, you will see that it is becoming more flexible. You'll next learn some ways to make your code more concise while keeping that flexibility!

2.1.4 Horoscope Bot

In our next example program, we'll explore creating a Horoscope Chatbot! In Chinese culture, it is said that if a person is born in a certain year, they will bear a certain zodiac sign (one of twelve animals), and exhibit some characteristics of that animal. This twelve-animal sequence repeats every twelve years, so people who were born in, say, 1996, 1984, 1972, or 1948 will all bear the Rat zodiac sign.

We can write a Horoscope chatbot that asks the user their year of birth and tells them their zodiac sign. You have already learned all the tools you need to be able to build this chatbot. (Hint: Use conditionals.) Challenge yourself and give it a try! Design the chatbot with comments first. We provide the years and their corresponding zodiac animals here.

Rat	1996, 1984, 1972, 1960, 1948
Ox	1997, 1985, 1973, 1961, 1949
Tiger	1998, 1986, 1974, 1962, 1950
Rabbit	1999, 1987, 1975, 1963, 1951
Dragon	2000, 1988, 1976, 1964, 1952
Snake	2001, 1989, 1977, 1965, 1953
Horse	2002, 1990, 1978, 1966, 1954
Goat	2003, 1991, 1979, 1967, 1955
Monkey	2004, 1992, 1980, 1968, 1956
Rooster	2005, 1993, 1981, 1969, 1957
Dog	2006, 1994, 1982, 1970, 1958
Pig	2007, 1995, 1983, 1971, 1959

You'll notice as we progress that you'll write longer code. Use the continuation character \ to continue a line of code onto the next line. It's considered good practice to keep each line of your code to under 80 characters.

Here is one possible solution, using only what we've learned so far.

```
1   # Horoscope Bot
2   # Author:
3   # Date:
4   # Description: The bot asks what year you are
5   # born and tells you your Chinese Zodiac sign.
6
7   # Greet the user
8   print("Hello! I'm the Horoscope Bot. \
9   Tell me, what year were you born?")
10
11  # Get users year of birth
12  birth_year = input()
13
14  # 1996/1984/1972/1960/1948 ==> Rat
15  if birth_year=="1996" or birth_year=="1984" \
16     or birth_year=="1972" or birth_year=="1960" \
17     or birth_year=="1948":
18     print("You were born in the Year of the Rat!")
19
20  # 1997/1985/1973/1961/1949 ==> Ox
21  elif birth_year=="1997" or birth_year=="1985" \
22     or birth_year=="1973" or birth_year=="1961" \
23     or birth_year=="1949":
24     print("You were born in the Year of the Ox!")
25
26  # 1998/1986/1974/1962/1950 ==> Tiger
27  elif birth_year=="1998" or birth_year=="1986" \
```

```
28    or birth_year=="1974" or birth_year=="1962" \
29    or birth_year=="1950":
30    print("You were born in the Year of the Tiger!")
31
32 # 1999/1987/1975/1963/1951 ==> Rabbit
33 elif birth_year=="1999" or birth_year=="1987" \
34   or birth_year=="1975" or birth_year=="1963" \
35   or birth_year=="1951":
36   print("You were born in the Year of the Rabbit!")
37
38 # 2000/1988/1976/1964/1952 ==> Dragon
39 elif birth_year=="2000" or birth_year=="1988" \
40   or birth_year=="1976" or birth_year == "1964" \
41   or birth_year=="1952":
42   print("You were born in the Year of the Dragon!")
43
44 # 2001/1989/1977/1965/1953 ==> Snake
45 elif birth_year=="2001" or birth_year=="1989" \
46   or birth_year=="1977" or birth_year=="1965" \
47   or birth_year=="1953":
48   print("You were born in the Year of the Snake!")
49
50 # 2002/1990/1978/1966/1954 ==> Horse
51 elif birth_year=="2002" or birth_year=="1990" \
52   or birth_year=="1978" or birth_year=="1966" \
53   or birth_year=="1954":
54   print("You were born in the Year of the Horse!")
55
56 # 2003/1991/1979/1967/1955 ==> Goat
57 elif birth_year=="2003" or birth_year=="1991" \
58   or birth_year=="1979" or birth_year=="1967" \
59   or birth_year=="1955":
60   print("You were born in the Year of the Goat!")
61
62 # 2004/1992/1980/1968/1956 ==> Monkey
63 elif birth_year=="2004" or birth_year=="1992" \
64   or birth_year=="1980" or birth_year=="1968" \
65   or birth_year=="1956":
66   print("You were born in the Year of the Monkey!")
67
68 # 2005/1993/1981/1969/1957 ==> Rooster
69 elif birth_year=="2005" or birth_year=="1993" \
70   or birth_year=="1981" or birth_year=="1969" \
71   or birth_year=="1957":
72   print("You were born in the Year of the Rooster!")
73
74 # 2006/1994/1982/1970/1958 ==> Dog
75 elif birth_year=="2006" or birth_year=="1994" \
76   or birth_year=="1982" or birth_year=="1970" \
```

```
77     or birth_year=="1958":
78     print("You were born in the Year of the Dog!")
79
80  # 2007/1995/1983/1971/1959 ==> Pig
81  elif birth_year=="2007" or birth_year=="1995" \
82     or birth_year=="1983" or birth_year=="1971" \
83     or birth_year=="1959":
84     print("You were born in the Year of the Pig!")
85
86  # Error handling
87  else:
88     print ("Please enter a year between 1948 and 2007.")
```

This code is very long. There are two ways we can improve this program to make it more concise, while still retaining our chatbot's interaction and functionality. The first way to simplify our code is to store our years in lists, and use the `in` keyword to check that what the user typed was one of the elements in the list. Here's how it would look.

```
 1  # Horoscope Bot
 2  # Author:
 3  # Date:
 4  # Description: The bot asks what year you are
 5  # born and tells you your Chinese Zodiac sign.
 6
 7  # Greet the user
 8  print("Hello! I'm the Horoscope Bot. \
 9  Tell me, what year were you born?")
10
11  # Get users year of birth
12  birth_year = input()
13
14  # 1996/1984/1972/1960/1948 ==> Rat
15  if birth_year in ["1996","1984","1972","1960","1948"]:
16     print("You were born in the Year of the Rat!")
17
18  # 1997/1985/1973/1961/1949 ==> Ox
19  elif birth_year in ["1997","1985","1973","1961","1949"]:
20     print("You were born in the Year of the Ox!")
21
22  # ...
23
24  # 2007/1995/1983/1971/1959 ==> Pig
25  elif birth_year in ["2007","1995","1983","1971","1959"]:
26     print("You were born in the Year of the Pig!")
27
28  # Error handling
29  else:
30     print ("Please enter a year between 1948 and 2007.")
```

You might notice this program only calculates for years between 1948 and 2007. How would you change it if you want to include more years?

There is another, even more concise way to calculate your Chinese horoscope instead of comparing the user's input to all the 60 years: using the modulo operator. We will learn about calculations with numbers later in the book, but if you'd like to get ahead, look up the modulo (remainder) operator for details. Hint: You will also need to find a way to convert the user input into a number for the modulo operator to work properly. If you prefer, come back to this challenge after completing the next chapter!

2.1.5   Review Questions

Time to test how much you understand the content in this chapter. It is okay to go back and review!

THEORY AND UNDERSTANDING

- How do we make a list in Python?
- What module do we need to import to randomly choose something from a list? How do you import this module to your code?
- How can we test smaller pieces of our Python code?
- What is concatenation?
- What does a dot after a module name do in Python?
- What is the only kind of symbol we can have in a variable name in Python?
- What does a conditional do?
- Is the `elif` part of a conditional mandatory? How about the `else` part?
- What is wrong with this code fragment?

```
1  if color = "purple":
2    print("Cool!")
```

SYNTAX SELF-CHECK

What do the following functions and keywords mean:

- `=`
- `+`
- `" "`
- `[ ]`
- `random.choice()`
- `import`
- `if/elif/else`
- `==, <, >, !=`
- `and, or, not`
- `True, False`

2.1.6   Practice Exercises

Now it's time for you to practice writing some code from scratch!

FORTUNE COOKIE GENERATOR

Write a fortune cookie generator that prints out a random fortune to the screen when the program is run. It must select from the following fortunes:

- You will have great success.
- You will become rich.
- You will find love.

```
Welcome to Fortune Cookie Generator!
You will become rich.
```

Figure 2.1 Printing a random fortune to the screen.

```
Welcome to Fortune Cookie Generator!
You will have great success.
```

Figure 2.2 Printing another random fortune to the screen in a different run.

COFFEE BOT

Write a CoffeeBot that asks if you would like cream. It should accept Yes/yes or No/no as inputs, and reply appropriately depending on the answer. If the user inputs anything else, it should repeat back their answer and say that it does not understand.

```
I'm CoffeeBot. Would you like cream with your coffee? (Yes/No)
Yes
Here's your coffee with cream.
```

Figure 2.3 User enters Yes

```
I'm CoffeeBot. Would you like cream with your coffee? (Yes/No)
No
Here's your coffee, no cream.
```

Figure 2.4 User enters No

```
I'm CoffeeBot. Would you like cream with your coffee? (Yes/No)
yes
Here's your coffee with cream.
```

Figure 2.5 User enters yes in lowercase.

```
I'm CoffeeBot. Would you like cream with your coffee? (Yes/No)
Maybe
Sorry, I don't know what Maybe means.
```

Figure 2.6 User enters something else.

2.1.7 Glossary

- **import**, the action of bringing in external functionalities (as modules) for the program to do something extra. This is also the keyword used in Python to tell the interpreter to perform the action.
- **functions**, bits of code that you can use to add functionality into your program. Some examples you have seen previously include print() to output something to the screen, input() to obtain input from the terminal, and random.choice() to randomly select an item from a list. Functions are great for code reuse and for simplifying your code. You'll learn more about using and even creating your own functions later in this book.
- **operators**, special symbols in programming where a computational operation is carried out by the program, for example, addition (+), comparison (<), etc. In most cases an operator needs to have two operands (e.g., two numbers for addition) to occur, but in some cases only one operand is needed (e.g., turning a positive number into a negative number).
- **assignment**, a common operation in programming where a variable is set to store the value it is given. Typically the operation is indicated by an equal symbol (=) and is different from the mathematical operation with the same symbol. In math, it means the expression on the left of = is the same as that on the right. But in programming, it means the variable shown on the left of = is set to the value calculated on the right.
- **conditional**, a programming construct that allows the program to execute different code based on the current state of the program (e.g., the value of a certain variable), that is, the condition in which the program is.
- **the \ operator**, called the "escape" character. In programming languages, there exist some special characters that are not available on a standard keyboard (e.g., the invisible carriage-return character to start new line of output) or that are used for other purposes (e.g., the double-quote character, ", to indicate start and end of a string), but are needed as part of the output. The presence of the \ character signifies that the character immediately after it should not be considered as its original value but one of those special characters (e.g., \n means the invisible carriage-return character, \ " means the double-quote character). In Python, if this character is used on its own (as a backslash), it is the "continuation character."

2.2 CHATBOTS WITH LOOPS

Congratulations! You have successfully created a few chatbots, some with personality, too. Now let's create a few more chatbots that are more advanced, including ones able to detect and recover from errors, and repeat themselves if needed. These are the building blocks of great interactive chatbots.

2.2.1 Learning Outcomes

At the end of this unit, you will be able to …

ADVANCED STRING METHODS

- apply useful methods from the string object appropriately, for example:

```
1  mystring.lower()
2  mystring.upper()
3  mystring.strip()
```

FOR-LOOPS

- use a `for`-loop to iterate over elements of a list

```
1  for variable in sequence:
2     ...
```

- create a list using variables (e.g., from user inputs) to iterate over

INTEGER BASICS

- create a variable of integer (`int`) type
- convert an integer into a string
- apply conversion to concatenate two strings when given an `int` and a string

ADVANCED BOOLEAN

- use within a Boolean expression the `in` keyword for (1) strings in a list and (2) characters in a string

ADVANCED CONDITIONAL STATEMENTS

- design and implement nested conditionals

TOOLS AND CODING PROCESS

You will also be able to ...

- use the REPL interactive console (or IDLE shell) to test methods and inspect variables
- describe the characteristics of good software: usable, pleasing to read, minimizing duplication, robust to errors
- continue to include a short description of the program in the header

- test a basic program for unexpected cases, interactively
- test smaller pieces of code by commenting out blocks
- explain the interpreter's role in catching errors

2.2.2   A Robust Bot

A requirement for an advanced chatbot is that it has to be **robust**. What does that mean?

What robust means in a chatbot is that it should be able to function even when an error occurs, for example, when the user has inputted something not recognized, a value does not match with what is expected, or some required resources are not available.

> There are three main kinds of errors in programming: (1) Syntax errors, caused by incorrect use of keywords/structures (e.g., typos); (2) semantic errors, caused by misunderstandings of how the program is expected to function; and (3) runtime errors, caused by incorrect inputs or other issues emerging during the execution of the program.

Let's look back at our How's It Going Bot.

```
1   # How's it going bot
2   # Author:
3   # Date:
4   # Description: This bot will ask you how it's
5   # going and reply based on your answer
6
7   # Ask user how it's going
8   print("How's it going?")
9
10  # Get the user's reply
11  reply = input()
12
13  # If they said Good,
14  # reply Good!
15  if reply == "Good" or reply == "good" or reply == "great":
16    print("Good!")
17
18  # Otherwise if they said Bad
19  # reply Oh no!
20  elif reply == "Bad":
21    print("Oh no!")
22
23  # Otherwise reply "I see..."
24  else:
25    print("I see...")
```

What happens if the user inputs, I'm good.? Our chatbot will reply, I see..., instead of what we would expect it to say (Good!). This is an example of a semantic error. Our program runs, but doesn't produce an expected or suitable result.

The reason why this error happens is that our bot is looking for complete matches in each of the if statements: it looks for Good, good, great, and Bad. Since the input begins with I'm and ends with . the chatbot treats it as different from good or the other related strings, and thus determines that the default action is the correct one.

To make our chatbot robust to additional characters, we need to let it know that it is OK to have a match *within* the input. In our last section, we discovered the in keyword, which allowed us to check whether a string was contained within a list of strings. In Python, we can use the in keyword also to see if a string is contained within another string.

Replace line 15 with the following code:

```
15  if "Good" in reply or "good" in reply or "great" in reply:
16      print("Good!")
```

Now if the user inputs I'm good. our chatbot will check if any of Good, good, and great is within the input, which is the case here, and say Good!

> The keyword in is a very useful keyword in Python and has different uses depending on what you use it with. Here we learn that we can use it to check if a string is within another string (i.e., is a "substring" of the other string). We will see other uses later in this book.

Now, what if the user is upset and inputs Very BAD!? Even with the in keyword our chatbot will not be able to reply Oh no! This is because besides the letters needing to be identical, the capitalization needs to be identical too. So BAD is treated as a different string from bad.

To make our chatbot robust to variations in capitalization we can first process the input to eliminate concerns of uppercase or lowercase letters. In Python, the method lower() converts all uppercase letters into lowercase letters (can you guess the name of the method that does the opposite?). Replace line 11 with the following code:

```
11  reply = input().lower()
```

> In programming languages, functions and methods are both bits of code that add functionalities. Functions are freestanding bits of code (e.g., input()), whereas methods are bits of code associated to something else that have to be used via the dot operator (e.g., random.choice()).

After the user inputs their response, Python applies the lower() method to the input, creating a version of the response where all the letters are in lowercase. Now we can update our How's It Going Bot into a more robust version:

```
 1  # How's it going bot (a more robust version)
 2  # Author:
 3  # Date:
 4  # Description: This bot will ask you how it's
 5  # going and reply based on your answer
 6
 7  # Ask user how it's going
 8  print("How's it going?")
 9
10  # Get the user's reply, all lowercase
11  reply = input().lower()
12
13  # If they said Good,
14  # reply Good!
15  if "good" in reply \
16  or "great" in reply:
17     print("Good!")
18
19  # Otherwise if they said Bad
20  # reply Oh no!
21  elif "bad" in reply:
22     print("Oh no!")
23
24  # Otherwise reply "I see..."
25  else:
26     print("I see...")
```

Try different inputs such as `Really great!` `Bad, bad, bad ...`, and `GOOD!!`

What if the user inputs something like `not good`? The current version of the chatbot is not robust against situations like this. We'll leave this as a challenge for you.

2.2.3   Food Bot

Our next example will combine together the various constructs we've learned so far. We'll create a Food Bot, which provides recommendations on where to find the best local cuisine.

Our Food Bot will ask the user about their favorite dish and suggest a place where their favorite food is served. As an example, let's start with Japanese food. You may be familiar with Japanese dishes like tempura, sushi, and sashimi. In this program, if the user inputs any one of these dishes, our chatbot recognizes that it is a type of Japanese food. Here, we use the `in` keyword again, as in our Horoscope Bot: if the right side of `in` is a list, Python will check if the value on the left side matches with any of the items in the list. This is very similar to asking the question: is something *in* the list?

Figure 2.7 Where do we go for food?

```
1   # Food Bot (Japanese food expert)
2   # Author:
3   # Date:
4
5   # Asks your favourite dish?
6   print("What's your favourite dish?")
7
8   # Gets your reply, e.g., tempura
9   favourite = input().lower()
10
11  # Create a list of Japanese foods, including
12  # tempura, sushi, sashimi
13  japanese_foods = ["tempura", "sushi", "sashimi"]
14
15  # If your favourite food is in the Japanese
16  # food list, then give a recommendation
17  if favourite in japanese_foods:
18      print("Oh! You should try Sushi Garden in Metrotown.")
19  else:
20      print("Sorry, not sure. You could always try Cactus Club!")
```

We have made our chatbot a bit more robust by accepting capitalization, so inputs like Tempura and SUSHI will still be matched with items in the list. What about inputs from someone who is really excited (e.g., Sushi!!) or indecisive (e.g., Sashimi ...?).

Inputs with punctuation marks will not be matched by our chatbot because the punctuation marks are treated as part of the string. We can use another method in Python called strip() that removes a selected set of characters in the front or at the back of a string. For example, strip(".?!") removes all the ., ?, and ! from the string. So if we replace line 9 with the following code, our chatbot will be now able to look past the punctuation marks.

```
9   favourite = input().lower().strip(".?!")
```

METHOD CHAINING

The replacement code above demonstrates a special way of using methods called *chaining*, where the output of one method is used as the input to the next method.

When the `input()` function reads in the user input, it produces a string variable storing the input. Then, it is used as an input for the `lower()` method (connected to it by a `.`) that produces another string variable that turns all the uppercase letters into lowercase letters. Finally, this string variable is used as an input for the `strip(".?!")` method to produce the resulting string variable with the leading and trailing `.`, `?`, and `!` removed.

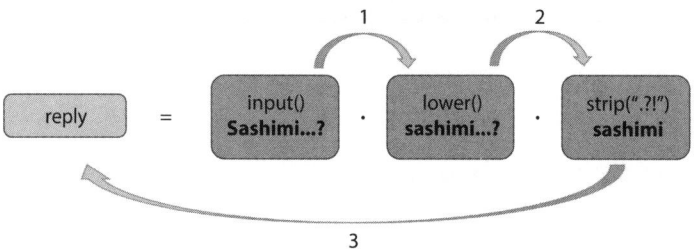

Figure 2.8 Method chaining goes from left to right.

Method chaining is useful for keeping your code concise. However, sometimes the order in which the methods are chained changes how the resulting string will look. For example, the results produced by the following two lines of code are different when the user inputs APPLE:

```
1  fruit_1 = input().lower().strip("a")
2  fruit_2 = input().strip("a").lower()
```

Can you guess what string would be contained in each of `fruit_1` and `fruit_2` after the code is run? Check in your Python IDE to see if you're right! All in all, when using method chaining, be cautious about the order of the methods. Create a few possible inputs to test your code, and check that the ordering gives you what you expect.

2.2.4 Measuring Things in Canada

In our next example, you will learn a more advanced form of branching, called **nested conditionals**.

Depending on where you live, you may use a specific system for measurement: the imperial system, the metric system, or both! For example, in France, people weigh steaks in grams (a metric unit), whereas in the US, people measure hamburgers in pounds (an imperial unit). In some places, like Canada, people use both depending on the situation. People who are new to Canada may need to use a decision tree like the one below to determine if they are going to use metric units or imperial units.

NESTED CONDITIONALS

```
1  # How to Measure Things in Canada
2  # Authors:
3  # Date:
```

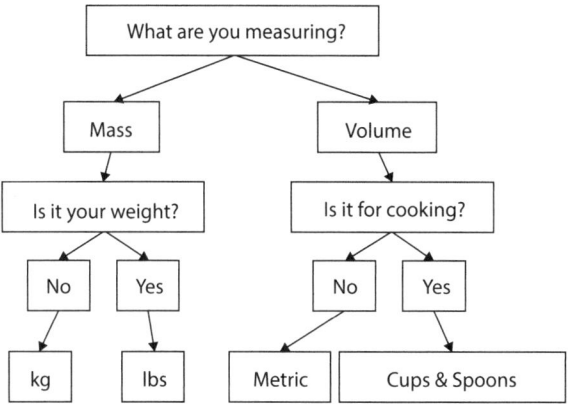

Figure 2.9 A decision tree for Canadians to determine which unit to use.

```
 4
 5  print("I can tell you how to do measurements in Canada!")
 6  measure = input("What are you measuring \
 7                       (mass/volume)? ").lower().strip(".!")
 8
 9  # Left branch - mass.
10  # If weight, lbs. Otherwise kg
11  if measure == "mass":
12    is_weight = input("Is it your weight?").lower()
13    if is_weight == "yes":
14      print("Use lbs.")
15    else:
16      print("Use kg.")
17
18  # Right branch - volume.
19  # If cooking, cups & spoons. Otherwise metric.
20  elif measure == "volume":
21    # TODO: Add this branch
22    pass
```

This sample code demonstrates a more complicated programming construct called "nested conditionals," where a conditional construct (the if-else statements between lines 13 and 16) is placed inside another conditional construct to further make a decision. In Python, it is indicated by indenting the statements, and therefore they are "nested." The flow goes like this:

If the user enters the word mass, then it further checks whether the user enters yes to the question, Is it your weight? This means that the checking of the answer to the question about weight only happens if the user entered the word mass in the beginning.

This mechanism allows the program to make decisions only when it makes sense. For example, if the user is trying to measure volume, it would not make sense to ask whether they want to measure their weight.

Line 22 uses the keyword pass to tell Python to do nothing if the user enters volume. It is there because Python requires at least one statement under each condition. Challenge yourself! Replace the pass keyword with a nested conditional to help the bot determine if the unit should be Metric or Cups & Spoons (Hint: Start by asking if what you're measuring is for cooking).

2.2.5   Bubble Tea Menu

Figure 2.10 A sample Bubble Tea menu.

In this section, you will learn about a construct called a **loop**!

Have you heard of bubble tea? Our next example will be themed on this tea-based beverage that comes in different flavours with tapioca pearls and can be served either hot or cold. Suppose you are creating a chatbot that shows the customer a menu of all the flavours being served.

We *could* technically use the following code to print the menu, and if we want to add more flavours we could copy/paste a few lines and modify the text:

```
 1  # Bubble Tea Menu (Version 1)
 2  # Author
 3  # Date
 4  # Prints a bubble tea menu
 5
 6  print("Mango milk")
 7  print("~~~~~~~~~~~~~")
 8  print("Taro milk")
 9  print("~~~~~~~~~~~~~")
10  print("Matcha milk")
11  print("~~~~~~~~~~~~~")
12  print("Oreo milk")
13  print("~~~~~~~~~~~~~")
14  print("Strawberry milk")
15  print("~~~~~~~~~~~~~")
16  print("Coconut milk")
17  print("~~~~~~~~~~~~~")
```

However, this code is somewhat unsatisfying because there is quite a bit of code duplication. Just as in English essays, we would prefer our code to be concise. Also, what if later we want to change the dividers from using ~ to #? Would we really have to change every single line that prints the dividers?

A BETTER WAY TO REPEAT CODE

We can reduce the number of lines of code by more than half by using a **loop**. Here is the process. First, write the code for one iteration, like this:

```
1  # Bubble Tea Menu (Version 2)
2  # Author:
3  # Date:
4  # Prints a bubble tea menu
5
6  print("Mango milk")
7  print("~~~~~~~~~~~~~")
```

Test to see if it works—it should, printing one flavour and one divider. Now, think about what (if anything) would change between the repetitions of your code. For example, here the flavour would change with each repetition, but the `milk` part would stay the same. So we can factor out the flavour element into a variable. Let's call the variable `flavour`.

```
1  # Bubble Tea Menu (Version 2)
2  # Author:
3  # Date:
4  # Prints a bubble tea menu
5
6  flavour = "Mango"
7  print(flavour + " milk")
8  print("~~~~~~~~~~~~~")
```

Now our code is becoming more flexible. How can we then make the flavour variable take on the different flavours, such as taro, matcha, etc.? Let's list out all the values that flavour could be (line 6):

```
1  # Bubble Tea Menu (Version 2)
2  # Author:
3  # Date:
4  # Prints a bubble tea menu
5
6  flavours = ["Mango", "Taro", "Matcha", "Oreo",
7              "Strawberry", "Coconut"]
8  flavour = "Mango"
9  print(flavour + " milk")
10 print("~~~~~~~~~~~~~")
```

Finally, in order for the variable `flavour` to take on the flavour values from the list, we use a for-loop programming construct. A for-loop has two parts that you can change, indicated here in italics: for *variable* in *sequence*.

The first part is *variable*, in this case `flavour`, and the second part is *sequence*, in this case the list `flavours`, which stores all the flavours you want the variable to take on.

Instead of setting `flavour` to Mango, let's allow the `for`-loop to automatically set `flavour` to all the values within the `flavours` list, one by one:

- Change line 8 from **flavour = "Mango"** to **for flavour in flavours:**
- Indent the loop body (lines 9 and 10), the section you want repeated

```
1   # Bubble Tea Menu (Version 2)
2   # Author:
3   # Date:
4   # Prints a bubble tea menu
5
6   flavours = ["Mango", "Taro", "Matcha", "Oreo",
7               "Strawberry", "Coconut"]
8   for flavour in flavours:
9     print(flavour + " milk")
10    print("~~~~~~~~~~~~~")
```

Notice how the bot prints the menu with all the flavours—all with just a few lines of code! Challenge: How how you can add more flavours to the menu? How would you change the way the divider looks?

2.2.6   Mind Reader Game

Let's combine what we have covered so far and create a chatbot that works as a game host.

The Mind Reader game is a two-player game where the first player reads a word and secretly enters the words they associate with it. For example, the player could associate the word "cat" with "fluffy," "cute," and "soft." The second player must then try to guess at least one of those words. If there is a match, both players win.

```
1   # Mind Reader Game
2   # Author:
3   # Date:
4   # This is a 2-player game.
5   # The 1st player reads a word and secretly
6   # enters 3 words they associate with it.
7   # The 2nd player must then try to guess at
8   # least one of the words.
9   # If it's a match, they win!
10
11  # Introduce the game
12  print("Welcome to Mind Reader")
13
14  # Ask the first player to enter 3 words
15  # associated with a given word
16  print("Player 1, enter 3 words you think \
17  of when I say cat:")
18
```

```
19  # Get the 3 words from the user
20  first_word = input("First word: ").lower()
21  second_word = input("Second word: ").lower()
22  third_word = input("Third word: ").lower()
23
24  # Clear the screen
25  print(100*"\n")
26
27  # Ask the 2nd player to guess
28  print("Player 2, what is one word you think \
29  Player 1 associates with cat?")
30  guess = input().lower()
31
32  # Check if they match and tell them if they win!
33  if guess in [first_word, second_word, third_word]:
34    print("You got it!")
35
36  # Otherwise, if they got it wrong
37  else:
38    print("No match! They said " + first_word + \
39    ", "+ second_word + " and " + third_word)
```

Line 25 prints 100 lines so that the words inputted by Player 1 will be hidden from Player 2. You can change 100 to an other number depending on how many new lines are needed to push their input out of the screen.

FOR-LOOPS WITH LISTS

As you can see, the chatbot asks Player 1 to input three associated words, and uses in to determine if Player 2 has correctly guessed any of those words. What if we want this game to repeat three times where a different word is used each time for Player 1 to associate?

If your answer is to use a for-loop, you are correct! To make it all work, we need to first provide the for-loop a sequence of words and factor out the part that gets changed every time it repeats. In this case, we create a list in line 15 and factor out the variable word in lines 22 and 34.

```
1  # Mind Reader Game (3 Rounds)
2  # Author:
3  # Date:
4  # This is a 2-player game.
5  # The 1st player reads a word and secretly
6  # enters 3 words they associate with it.
7  # The 2nd player must then try to guess at
8  # least one of the words.
9  # If it's a match, they win!
```

```
10
11   # Introduce the game
12   print("Welcome to Mind Reader")
13
14   # Make a list of words
15   word_list = ["cat", "dog", "apple"]
16
17   # Loop through all the items in words
18   for word in word_list:
19     # Ask the first player to enter 3 words
20     # associated with a given word
21     print ("Player 1, enter 3 words you think \
22     of when I say " + word)
23
24     # Get the 3 words from the user
25     first_word = input("First word: ").lower()
26     second_word = input("Second word: ").lower()
27     third_word = input("Third word: ").lower()
28
29     # Clear the screen
30     print(100*"\n")
31
32     # Ask the 2nd player to guess
33     print("Player 2, what is one word you think \
34     Player 1 associates with " + word + "?")
35     guess = input().lower()
36
37     # Check if they match and tell them if they win!
38     if guess in [first_word, second_word, third_word]:
39       print("You got it!")
40
41     # Otherwise, if they got it wrong
42     else:
43       print("No match! They said " + first_word + \
44       ", "+ second_word + " and " + third_word)
```

FOR-LOOPS WITH RANGE

In the code sample above, the number of repetitions of the for-loop is the same as the number of items in the list that it uses (and in the same order). Sometimes we do not have such a list and we want the for-loop to repeat a fixed number of times. What can we do then?

Let's demonstrate by adding one more feature to the game so that, besides repeating three times, it draws a word from a list of more than three words randomly each time.

To control how many times the for-loop repeats, we replace the list with the function call range(n), where *n* is the number of repetitions (see line 19). We add a few more possible words to the list of words and use the random function we covered earlier to randomly choose a word (see line 22).

```python
1   # Mind Reader Game (3 Rounds with random words)
2   # Author:
3   # Date:
4   # This is a 2-player game.
5   # The 1st player reads a word and secretly
6   # enters 3 words they associate with it.
7   # The 2nd player must then try to guess at
8   # least one of the words.
9   # If it's a match, they win!
10
11  # Introduce the game
12  print("Welcome to Mind Reader")
13
14  # Make a list of words
15  word_list = ["cat", "dog", "apple", "hot",
16              "coffee", "sport", "snow"]
17
18  # do 3 rounds
19  for i in range(3):
20    # Ask the first player to enter 3 words
21    # associated with a randomly selected word
22    word = random.choice(word_list)
23    print("Player 1, enter 3 words you think of when I \
24        say " + word)
25
26    # Get the 3 words from the user
27    first_word = input("First word: ").lower()
28    second_word = input("Second word: ").lower()
29    third_word = input("Third word: ").lower()
30
31    # Clear the screen
32    print(100*"\n")
33
34    # Ask the 2nd player to guess
35    print("Player 2, what is one word you think Player 1 \
36        associates with " + word + "?")
37    guess = input().lower()
38
39    # Check if they match and tell them if they win!
40    if guess in [first_word, second_word, third_word]:
41      print("You got it!")
42
43    # Otherwise, if they got it wrong
44    else:
45      print("No match! They said " + first_word + \
46      ", "+ second_word + " and " + third_word)
```

> The variable **i** in the for-loop stores a number each time the for-loop repeats!
> If you use print() to show its value, you'll see it goes from 0, 1, 2, … to n-1.
> What range does is it generates a sequence of numbers from 0 to n-1 for the
> for-loop to set its variable to, causing it to repeat n times. Challenge: What if you
> want to print Round 1, Round 2, and so on for the repetition?

2.2.7   Review Questions

Time to test how much you understand the content in this chapter. It is okay to go back and
review!

THEORY AND UNDERSTANDING

- What coding construct did we learn that can help us avoid duplicating code? What
  keywords do we need?
- True or false? Methods can be chained from left to right.
- What would the following code output?

```
1   for i in ["0", "1", "2"]:
2       print(i)
```

- How could we use the range(n) function to print the same thing as the code snippet
  above?
- What would the following code output?

```
1   print("!.?blah".strip("!.h").upper())
```

- The following code snippet contains some redundant (unnecessary) code. What would
  the code output? How could you simplify it?

```
1   foods = ["Burger", "Taco", "Tempura"]
2   print("Tempura".lower().upper() in foods)
```

SYNTAX SELF-CHECK

What do the following functions and keywords mean:

- mystring.lower(), mystring.upper(), mystring.strip()
- in (strings/lists)
- for <var> in <sequence>:
- str(...), int(...)
- nested conditionals, i.e.,
  if <condition>:
        if <condition>:
  else:
- range(4), range(1,5), range(1,10,2)

2.2.8   Practice Exercises

CODING

Now it's time for you to practice by writing some code. When you are finished, you can go to the Solutions section on our companion website to compare your answers with ours. Note that there can be many answers to the same question, so don't worry if your code is not exactly the same as ours. For now, the important thing is that your code produces the results you expect.

NEW YEAR'S BOT

Write a New Year's Bot that counts down from 10 to 1. It should use a `for`-loop and each number should be on a new line. At the end of the countdown, it should output `Happy new year!`.

```
10
9
8
7
6
5
4
3
2
1
Happy new year!
>
```

Figure 2.11 Count down from 10 to 1 and say `Happy new year!`.

First write your solution using a list as the `for`-loop sequence, then write another solution using range as the `for`-loop sequence.

WHICH SIDE BOT

Write a Which Side Bot that decides if you can be on the Dark side, or the Light side. The requirement to be a Dark Lord is pretty easy. If you like capes or the colour red, then you're in! Otherwise it will recommend you to the Light side. Your bot should be robust to uppercase/lowercase answers of yes and no.

```
I will decide if you can join the Dark Side.
Is red your favourite colour? yes
Do you like capes? yes
Dark side it is!
>
```

Figure 2.12 Deciding that the user can be on the Dark side.

```
I will decide if you can join the Dark Side.
Is red your favourite colour? yes
Do you like capes? no
Dark side it is!
>
```

Figure 2.13 Deciding that the user can be on the Dark side.

```
I will decide if you can join the Dark Side.
Is red your favourite colour? no
Do you like capes? yes
Dark side it is!
>
```

Figure 2.14 Deciding that the user can be on the Dark side.

```
I will decide if you can join the Dark Side.
Is red your favourite colour? no
Do you like capes? no
Light side, I see.
>
```

Figure 2.15 Deciding that the user can be on the Light side.

2.2.9   Glossary

- **robust**, a quality of a program being not prone to failing when an error occurs (e.g., invalid user input). This is typically achieved by careful planning and writing code that handles errors when they occur.
- **chaining**, the ability to apply multiple operations (methods) one after the other by feeding the result of one operation to the next as input. This makes the code compact and concise.
- **method**, similar to functions; methods are bits of code that add functionalities to the program. However, they are applied to something that is in the program (typically a variable) and thus have to be associated to something else via the dot operator (e.g., input().lower() turns all the characters to lowercase in the string variable produced by input()).
- **loop**, a programming construct that repeats the same piece of code multiple times as determined by a condition or a lookup sequence. Together with variables that get changed every time the code repeats, one can write very compact code that does sophisticated tasks (e.g., access a collection of data once and only once).

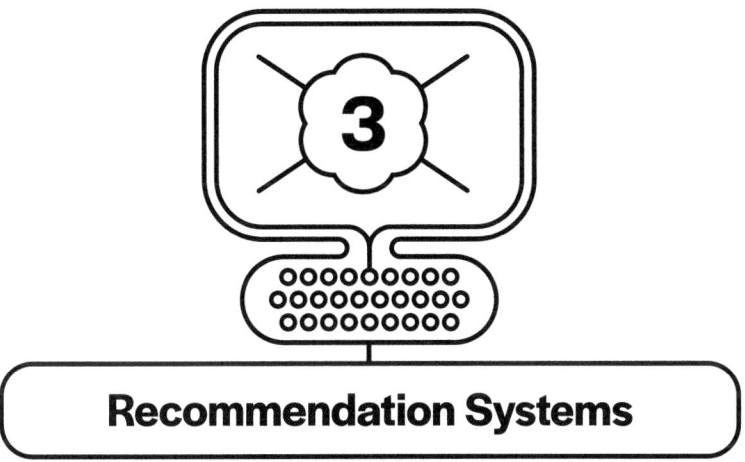

Recommendation Systems

Many services nowadays collect user data and provide relevant information as recommendations. In this chapter you'll write programs that use some basic matching techniques to do just that!

Recommendation systems such as Netflix's and Amazon's "You might also like" features are a great way to help people discover new things they may like. Under the hood, it's statistics and looking for matches. Today's recommendation system software uses large datasets and machine learning to generate recommendations. Their advanced AI algorithms are outside the scope of this book, but in this chapter you'll learn how to write chatbots that provide recommendations to their users based on the information they collect and store in files.

The chatbot programs that you'll be writing include:

- Popular Cafe Finder
- Chip Rater
- Movie Rater
- Favourite Pets Finder
- Common Interests Finder
- Similar People Finder

Through writing these chatbot programs in Python, you'll learn about different data types and conversion between them, list indexing, and reading from files. You will also learn about how to write good code.

CS topics in this unit:

- Avoiding code duplication
- Loops with ranges
- Accumulator variables
- String/`int`/`float` data types
- Type conversion
- Length
- Division
- Order of operators
- Splitting, indexing, and comparing lists

- Opening and reading files
- Comparison operators
- Nested loops

3.1   POPULARITY CONTEST

How do you know something is the most popular? You would probably start with a few options, maybe ask others about their opinions or do a little bit of research yourself, then decide based on your findings.

Computers do exactly the same by collecting information as data points, processing them, and producing an answer by choosing the option that satisfies some criteria the most.

3.1.1   Learning Outcomes

At the end of this unit, you will be able to …

ARITHMETIC AND CONVERSION

- use integers and floats and manipulate them in variables
- initialize a variable of type integer
- convert strings to integer type (including from user input)
- know that division of integers converts type to `float`
- perform arithmetic operations on numbers

ACCUMULATION PATTERN

- apply the accumulator pattern (including initialization) and the `+=` shortcut
- use the accumulator pattern with other arithmetic operators

FOR-LOOP WITH RANGE

- use the `range` function with arguments that are variables (not only numbers)
- know that a loop is a way to reduce duplication of code

3.1.2   Popular Cafe Finder

Suppose you are going for a coffee break with a few friends and you want to find the best cafe to go to. There are three nearby options: Starbucks, Artiggiano, and Tim Hortons. Here we are going to write a chatbot that asks five people about their opinions and displays the results.

```
1   # Most Popular Cafe Finder
2   # Author:
3   # Date:
4   # A survey to deduce the most popular cafe
5   # Starbucks - an international cafe
6   # Tim Hortons - a Canadian cafe
7   # Artiggiano - a local cafe
8   # The cafe which gets the most votes is the most popular
9
10  # Initialize tallies to 0
```

```
11  starbucks_tally = 0
12  tim_hortons_tally = 0
13  artiggiano_tally = 0
14
15  for i in range(5):
16    # Ask the user what their favourite cafe is
17    favourite_cafe = input(What's your favourite of
18  Starbucks, Tim Hortons, Artiggiano? ").lower()
19
20    # add 1 to the matching tally
21    if favourite_cafe == "starbucks":
22      starbucks_tally = starbucks_tally + 1
23
24    elif favourite_cafe == "tim hortons":
25      tim_hortons_tally = tim_hortons_tally + 1
26
27    elif favourite_cafe == "artiggiano":
28      artiggiano_tally = artiggiano_tally + 1
29
30  # Print out how many people who like each one
31  print("Starbucks:", starbucks_tally)
32  print("Tim Hortons:", tim_hortons_tally)
33  print("Artiggiano:", artiggiano_tally)
```

In the above code, we first create three tally variables, each storing the number of votes cast towards the cafe it represents. Each of these variables, such as starbucks_tally, contains an integer. As opposed to strings, an integer is a data type used in computer science to store whole numbers. Since there are no votes in the beginning, we initialize the tally values to 0.

A variable containing "0" is different from a variable containing 0. When the number 0 is surrounded by quotes, it is a string containing the character 0. When 0 is without quotes, it is an integer data type. This is important to know, because "1"+"2" becomes "12" whereas 1+ 2 becomes 3!

The for-loop repeats the question five times to get five votes from different people. Each time we get an answer, we match with the three options and increase the matching option's tally by 1. Note that the + symbol previously was performing concatenation to glue two strings together. Since our tally variables are integers, the + symbol now performs an addition!

A shorthand way to add to a variable, and reduce repetition in our code, is to use the += construct. See below how we have replaced lines 22, 25, and 28. The += 1 expression is a compound assignment that is a shorthand for "increment the original value by 1."

```
1  # Most Popular Cafe Finder
2  # Author:
3  # Date:
```

```
 4  # A survey to deduce the most popular cafe
 5  # Starbucks - an international cafe
 6  # Time Hortons - a Canadian cafe
 7  # Artiggiano - a local cafe
 8  # The cafe which gets the most votes is the most popular
 9
10  # Initialize tallies to 0
11  starbucks_tally = 0
12  tim_hortons_tally = 0
13  artiggiano_tally = 0
14
15  for i in range(5):
16      # Ask the user what their favourite cafe is
17      favourite_cafe = input(What's your favourite of
18  Starbucks, Tim Hortons, Artiggiano? ").lower()
19
20      # add 1 to the matching tally
21      if favourite_cafe == "starbucks":
22          starbucks_tally += 1
23
24      elif favourite_cafe == "tim hortons":
25          tim_hortons_tally += 1
26
27      elif favourite_cafe == "artiggiano":
28          artiggiano_tally += 1
29
30  # Prints out how many people who like each one
31  print("Starbucks:", starbucks_tally)
32  print("Tim Hortons:", tim_hortons_tally)
33  print("Artiggiano:", artiggiano_tally)
```

When the chatbot gets the votes from all five people, it outputs the total number of votes for each cafe. We can use another form of print(), which uses a comma between values of different types. This allows us to easily output a string followed by a number.

We can also process the tallies and produce percentages for each cafe. This requires us to use additional mathematical constructs: multiplication (*) and division (/). The usage of these mathematical operators follows the order of operations you are likely familiar with from calculators.

It is important to know that, when performing division in Python, your result will end up in a data type called a **floating point** number. Floating point numbers, sometimes called floats, store decimal numbers in a computer.

```
1  # Most Popular Cafe Finder
2  # Author:
3  # Date:
4  # A survey to deduce the most popular cafe
5  # Starbucks - an international cafe
6  # Time Hortons - a Canadian cafe
```

```
 7   # Artiggiano - a local cafe
 8   # The cafe which gets the most votes is the most popular
 9
10   # Initialize tallies to 0
11   starbucks_tally = 0
12   tim_hortons_tally = 0
13   artiggiano_tally = 0
14
15   for i in range(5):
16     # Ask the user what their favourite cafe is
17     favourite_cafe = input(What's your favourite of
18   Starbucks, Tim Hortons, Artiggiano? ").lower()
19
20     # add 1 to the matching tally
21     if favourite_cafe == "starbucks":
22       starbucks_tally += 1
23
24     elif favourite_cafe == "tim hortons":
25       tim_hortons_tally += 1
26
27     elif favourite_cafe == "artiggiano":
28       artiggiano_tally += 1
29
30   # Prints out the percentage of people who like
31   # each one, up to 2 decimal places
32   print("Starbucks: ", starbucks_tally/5*100)
33   print("Tim Hortons: ", tim_hortons_tally/5*100)
34   print("Artiggiano: ", artiggiano_tally/5*100)
```

Tip: Use print() statements in your code to check the values of variables. For example, if you want to check the value of i, add a temporary print(i) within the loop. This method of checking values of variables is also called tracing. Remember to remove the temporary code when you're done!

Try out the program, with different user inputs to your survey, and check the results! One issue you might find with your program is that the output values may result in many trailing decimal places. How could we round the number to, say, two decimal places?

We can use the format() method to adjust how the text is being printed: the {:.2f} means "replace the contents of the curly braces with a floating point value with two places after the decimal." This is particularly useful when we have values that have a lot of decimal places and we only want to print a fixed number of them. This is an advanced feature of Python, and details of format() are outside the scope of this book.

```
1   # Most Popular Cafe Finder
2   # Author:
3   # Date:
```

```
4   # A survey to deduce the most popular cafe
5   # Starbucks - an international cafe
6   # Time Hortons - a Canadian cafe
7   # Artiggiano - a local cafe
8   # The cafe which gets the most votes is the most popular
9
10  # Initialize tallies to 0
11  starbucks_tally = 0
12  tim_hortons_tally = 0
13  artiggiano_tally = 0
14
15  for i in range(5):
16    # Ask the user what their favourite cafe is
17    favourite_cafe = input(What's your favourite of
18  Starbucks, Tim Hortons, Artiggiano? ").lower()
19
20    # add 1 to the matching tally
21    if favourite_cafe == "starbucks":
22      starbucks_tally += 1
23
24    elif favourite_cafe == "tim hortons":
25      tim_hortons_tally += 1
26
27    elif favourite_cafe == "artiggiano":
28      artiggiano_tally += 1
29
30  # Prints out the percentage of people who like
31  # each one, up to 2 decimal places
32  print("Starbucks: {:.2f}%".format(starbucks_tally/5*100))
33  print("Tim Hortons: {:.2f}%".format(tim_hortons_tally/5*100))
34  print("Artiggiano: {:.2f}%".format(artiggiano_tally/5*100))
```

Challenge: How would you modify the code in our program to make it robust to extra punctuation, such as a user typing `Starbucks!!`?

3.1.3   Chip Rater

Psychologists and experimenters often have to run surveys to see how people perceive the world. Sometimes the surveys are quite funny! In this example program, you will learn more about the integer type and practice creating another survey.

In 2008, Ig Nobel Prize winners Massimiliano Zampini and Charles Spence did a study on how the sound of potato chips being eaten affects people's perception of the chips' crispiness. They discovered that just by hearing a louder crunching sound, chips would seem more crispy!

Let's imagine you are Zampini and Spence's assistant. You need to write a chatbot to ask the study's participants about their rating of the chips. How would you do it?

Here is a sample code that asks one person to rate three different characteristics of the chip, and calculates an overall rating:

```
1   # Chip Rater
2   # Author:
3   # Date:
4   # To rate chips from 1-5 on various factors
5   # such as crispiness, taste, etc.
6   # and get an overall average score out of 5.
7
8   # Greet the participant
9   print("Welcome to our Chip Rater experiment.")
10  print("Please answer three questions on a scale of 1-5.")
11
12  # Make a list of questions about chip goodness
13  questions = ["How crispy are the chips? ",
14               "How would you rate the taste? ",
15               "How would you rate the packaging? "]
16
17  # Initialize overall score
18  score = 0
19
20  # For each question, get their response out of 5
21  # and convert it to an int
22  for question in questions:
23    rating = input(question)
24    score = score + int(rating)
25
26  # Calculate final overall score
27  # by taking the sum of all ratings
28  # and dividing by number of questions.
29  print("Overall score: " + str(score/len(questions)))
```

In the above code, we call the function int() in line 24 to convert the user input into an integer data type. This is necessary because the value stored in the variable rating comes from the input() function, which produces a string data type; and we cannot add an integer (the variable score) and a string.

Similarly, in line 29 we use the function str() to convert the result from a division operation, which is a numerical data type, into a string data type so it can be concatenated with "Overall score". Note also how we use the len() function to find out the number of questions. The len() function gives us the length of the list. This is a much better method than hard-coding the number 3 as the denominator, because if new questions are added to our questions list, the denominator will remain correct.

Here we continue seeing the Python data type that represents a number with decimals, the **float** data type. The **float** data type is very useful to maintain the precision of a number when there are decimals. Together with **int** and **string**, these three data types allow a wide range of programs to be created.

3.1.4   Movie Rater

In our previous code example, on finding the most popular nearby cafe to go to, we used a number of variables to store the tallies for the options: starbucks_tally, tim_hortons_tally, and artiggiano_tally.

This works well with a small number of options. What if we have more options? It will become harder to keep track of the variables, and if we want to print the results we might have to type a lot of code (and the more we type the more likely we are to make mistakes and make the code harder to modify).

Python provides an effective way to store pairs of values, similar to how it stores individual values in a list. It is called **dictionary**. In a dictionary, each item is a pair indicated by its key (think about label) and its value. Using our Popular Cafe Finder example, we could have a dictionary of three items, using the cafe names as the keys and starting with the value 0 for each of them.

Let's use another example here. Let's say we wish to write a Movie Rater chatbot that asks five people about their movie preference and displays the results. To keep it simple, we use three movies: Frozen, X-Men, and Harry Potter.

```
1   # Movie Rater with Dictionaries
2   # Author:
3   # Date:
4   # Asks 5 people for their movie ratings
5   # and tracks them using dictionaries
6
7   # Initialize a dictionary of movies
8   movies = {"frozen": 0,
9             "x-men": 0,
10            "harry potter": 0}
11
12  # Ask 5 people for their movie preference
13  for i in range(5):
14    preference = input("Which movie is your \
15                  favourite out of Frozen, X-Men \
16                  or Harry Potter? ").lower().strip(" .!")
17
18    # Add 1 to the appropriate movie
19    movies[preference] += 1
20
21  # Print out the results using a loop
22  for movie in movies:
23    print(movie, movies[movie]) # Name and tally
```

Dictionaries provide a number of advantages over individual variables as well as lists:

- we can come up with a meaningful name for the tallies (movies);
- when referring to a pair in the dictionary, we can use the key of the pair, instead of a number in a list.

Thus, instead of using if/elif/else statements to determine which tally to add to, we can directly use the user input as key to refer to the pair and access its value (line 19).

In addition, the for-loop programming construct also accepts a dictionary as its *sequence* part and extracts the key of each pair in each iteration (lines 22 and 23). This is particularly useful when we have a lot of pairs to access (we can also extract keys directly via the keys() method of the dictionary).

Next, let's continue to improve our program. For instance, you'll notice that when you run the program above, it outputs the movie without capitalization. We can use a Python string method capitalize(), which will make the first letter in the string uppercase. Secondly, the example below (line 23) shows another way to output our results, using concatenation and conversion of the numeric tally to a string type using str(). By converting the number to a string type, we can concatenate the two strings together.

```
1   # Movie Rater with Dictionaries
2   # Author:
3   # Date:
4   # Asks 5 people for their movie ratings
5   # and tracks them using dictionaries
6
7   # Initialize a dictionary of movies
8   movies = {"frozen": 0,
9            "x-men": 0,
10           "harry potter": 0}
11
12  # Ask 5 people for their movie preference
13  for i in range(5):
14    preference = input("Which movie is your \
15                      favourite out of Frozen, X-Men \
16                      or Harry Potter? ").lower().strip(" .!")
17
18    # Add 1 to the appropriate movie
19    movies[preference] += 1
20
21  # Print out the results using a loop
22  for movie in movies:
23    print(movie.capitalize() + ": " + str(movies[movie]))
```

The ability to refer to a pair in the dictionary using the key of the pair makes our code clearer, as we can come up with something that accurately describes the pair. What happens if we try to access the value of a pair with a key that does not exist, or is typed incorrectly? If there is no pair in a dictionary with that key, Python will generate a KeyError indicating that the key does not exist in the dictionary and terminate the program.

To make our program more robust, we could include a conditional check using the in keyword. Replace line 19 with the following code:

```
1   if movie in movies:
2     movies[preference] += 1
3   else:
4     print("Please type Frozen, X-Men, or Harry Potter")
```

Another way is to make use of a feature of dictionary that automatically adds a pair to itself when the key is not found in the dictionary. Instead of the code above, replace line 19 with the following code:

```
1  if movie in movies:
2    movies[preference] += 1
3  else:
4    # if the key is not there, add a new pair
5    movies[preference] = 1
```

A new pair will be added to the movies dictionary with the initial value 1 (because the user has just cast a vote for that movie).

> The dictionary data type is very useful for storing an unordered collection of items and is not limited to just numbers (lists and strings, for example,). It also provides a number of functions to access the keys and values, and to modify itself by adding or removing pairs. While dictionaries are relatively advanced, we encourage you to investigate what they offer!

Another technique we can use is by introducing two "parallel lists," where we use one list to store tally options (names), and another list to store the tallies (numbers). This allows us to use the same index in the for-loop to access both lists in parallel. Using our Popular Cafe Finder example, we can have one list storing the cafe options (Starbucks, Tim Hortons, Artiggiano) and another list storing the tallies (0, 0, 0—initially). Then the index 0 will allow us to access the first option (Starbucks) and the corresponding first tally in the other list. This technique is often used to simulate the behaviour of Python's dictionaries in programming languages that do not have it.

3.1.5   Review Questions

Time to test how much you understand the content in this chapter. It is okay to go back and review!

THEORY AND UNDERSTANDING

- What do you need to do to numeric input before performing calculations on it?
- What are two data types for numbers? What's the difference between them?
- Which function could you use to get the number of elements in a list?
- How would you initialize a variable called tally to 0?
- How would you add 1 to a variable tally that was already initialized to 0?
- What keyword do you use to convert an integer into a string?
- What will this code output?

```
1  print( 3 / 3)
```

- What is the data type of the variable mystery in the code below? wonder?

```
1   mystery = 0
2   wonder = 0.
```

- What does the following Python code print as the first line?

```
1   for i in range(10,0,-1):
2     print("{:.2f} dollars".format(i*1/10))
```

- Will this code run? If not, how can you fix it?

```
1   score = 10
2   print("Your score is " + score)
```

- What is the data type being used to store numbers in the code snippet below? What will nums [2] be if the user inputs 3?

```
1   x = int(input())
2   nums = {}
3   for i in range(x):
4     nums[i] = "o"*i
```

SYNTAX SELF-CHECK

What do the following functions and keywords mean?

- `type(17)`
- `type(0.0)`
- `type("xoxo")`
- `type([1, 2, 3])`
- `type(True)`
- `2 ** 2`
- `3 * 4`
- `5 - 3`
- `4 + 4`
- `5 / 3`
- `5 // 3`
- `12 % 5`
- `x = 1`
- `x = x+1`
- `x += 1`
- `int(4.3)`
- `float("123.45")`
- `str(12.3)`
- `len(myList)`
- `mylist[0]`
- `print("Number: :.3f".format(myfloat))`

- `emptyDicto = {}`
- `dicto = {"element1": 0}`
- `dicto["element1"] = 2`

3.1.6   Practice Exercises

CODING

Now it's time for you to practice by writing some code. When you are done, you can go to the Solutions section on our companion website to compare your answers with ours. Note that there can be many answers to the same question, so don't worry if yours are not the same as ours. The important things are that they produce the same results, and that you are able to tell where the differences are and why both answers work.

OLYMPIC JUDGING

Write an **Olympic Judging** program that outputs the average score from five different judges. Each score is out of 10 points maximum. Half points (e.g., 7.5) are allowed. The program should take five inputs and output the final average score.

Here is a sample run:

Figure 3.1 Displaying the average score from five different judges.

FUTURE AGE

Write a **Future Age** program that asks your age and outputs how old you'll be 30 years (three decades) from now.

Here are two sample runs:

Figure 3.2 The user will be 40 if they are 10 now.

Figure 3.3 The user will be 65 if they are 35 now.

FAST FOOD ORDER

Write a **Fast Food Order** program that takes your order and outputs the total cost. It firsts asks if you want a burger for $5. It then asks if you want fries for $3. It outputs the total with 14% tax.

Your solution should initialize a prices dictionary with two items (burgers and fries) and their prices ($5 and $3, respectively), and offer all the items along with their prices. The total with tax should be outputted with two decimal places.

The program should be robust to accept yes/no with any combination of capitalization.

Here are two sample runs:

Figure 3.4 Just burger with tax is $5.70.

Figure 3.5 Both burger and fries with tax cost $9.12.

3.1.7 Glossary

- **compound assignment**, the combination of an operation on a variable and an assignment operation on that variable. For example, `i += 1` is a combination of the operation `i + 1` and the assignment of the result to the variable `i`. It is equivalent to the expression `i = i + 1`. Other compound assignments include `-=`, `*=`, `/=`, `//=`.
- **string formatting**, a way to specify how strings are being printed to the display. The format is described inside `{` and `}` and begins with `:` instead of the `%` in older versions of Python. The method `format` is then called by providing the values being printed. For details refer to https://docs.python.org/3/library/string.html.
- **casting**, an operation converting a variable's data type into another data type, also known as *type conversion*. This operation allows values to be used by operations expecting a different data type. For example, a variable returned by `input()` is of the string data type. In order to perform mathematical operations on it, it needs to be cast into a numerical data type (e.g., `int` or `float`). Sometimes Python performs casting automatically, but other times you will have to tell it what to do by calling the type conversion function explicitly.
- **parallel lists**, a technique where two lists of the same length are used to store options and their corresponding values. This allows the use of one index to efficiently access corresponding values in a large group of options.

3.2 FINDING YOUR MATCH

In the previous sections we explained how to write chatbots that collect data and provide recommendations based on counting tallies from a few users.

A more sophisticated recommendation system would do more than just asking for a few votes. Instead, it looks into hundreds or thousands of records and look for patterns and matches.

In this section we explain how to write chatbots that read data from files with thousands of entries and provide recommendations based on those data.

3.2.1 Learning Outcomes

At the end of this unit, you will be able to …

WORKING WITH TEXT FILES

- know the difference between binary files and plain text files (both can be used to store data, but differently)
- open and read lines from a text file
- open and write lines to a text file

INDEXING AND SLICING STRINGS AND LISTS

- access specific elements of a list using indexing/slicing
- access specific characters in a string using indexing/slicing

ADVANCED CODING STRUCTURES

- perform comparisons between numbers, taking into account the order of operators (operator precedence)
- perform comparisons between strings
- understand and use a nested `for`-loop (e.g., find common elements between two lists)
- apply accumulation pattern for strings and lists (previously was done only for numbers)

3.2.2   Data Files

Before we go into the details of writing our chatbots, let's take some time to understand how data are stored in files.

We use files to store our data because they allow us to keep records of data even when the programs are not running and the computers are off. We can also share the data with others by sending them these files.

Most files are stored in either a very compact way (binary files), or a more human-readable way (plain text files). Opening a binary file in a text editor application will result in strange characters being displayed, as the content is not designed to be readable by humans. However, if you open a plain text file, you will be able to see its content with the character set we recognize.

```
PK<0x03><0x04>
<0x00><0x00><0x00><0x00><0x00><0x00>??Z<0x00><0x00><0x00><0x00><0x00><0x00><0x00><0x00><0x00><0x00><0x00>
<0x00><0x00><0x00><0x00><0x00> }?Z<0x00><0x00><0x00><0x00><0x00><0x00><0x00><0x00><0x00><0x00><0x00
*?<0x01>? `@P2(7D??$<0x15><0x10>?????+???ₒ=U]]??????]??u???e*<0x18>L?<0x1a><0x06>?"???`?2
r<0x10><0x00><0x0e><0x00>?????4<0x02>?Cш?<0x18>?#<0x11><0x00>?<0x08>C?(?<0x05><0x12>??????<0x07><0x
1??<0x18>?p?>X)<0x0c>=D???b<0x05><0x16>?<0x10>ρ}2?,$???? E[??<0x00>?2<0x18>%HI^?<0x16>??!??;<0x1d>0
?? <0x01><0x04>?xw=<0x01>$<0x07>?<0x1e>?<0x16>?T<0x14>???<0x01>?^ws??P9?8<0x1e>????T?8r7<0x7f>?<0x1
??A<0x00> o<0x06>??"<0x1a>?W?ph?K"??qh<0x7f>"?<0x05>?<0x0b>??<0x13>?<0x01>8?`?+?<0x0f>???%<0x11>???
1??<0x11>*<0x08>A??&?{<0x15>????<0x0b>?2K?<0x16>ı;<0x05>?!?_d?<0x02>)A
?????w???<???,??<0x1b>?<0x17>    AR?d?x?h?????_??<0x14>e?<0x17>.?K<0x19>???ɳ\<0x06>??<0x04>?
<0x06>?<0x00>?7?;Im????<0x07><0x10>6^e'<0x07><0x1c>?<0x03>&j[??&?0yVN?a<0x1e>??<0x14>%]?Z<0x1c><0x0
?S???`???@W????
?n??c???v`i~??J?j? ??9e<0x03>;*?    .^?????#Mv?58<0x7f>n%??<0x10>8??xl<0x12>u?<0x13>X??;?b<0x03><0
<0x17>F?|w0??<0x08>?-f??{??y<0x01>\:?N????<0x7f>jL<0x17>???<0x04>l)??m??M??U]V0h?<0x12>???|??5?%?%&
<0x04>?<0x7f>?M?<0x05>&w???????T?+=
```

Figure 3.6 The content in a binary file. Only computers can read it.

We can write chatbots to read both types of files. But for simplicity, here we only focus on plain text files. To proceed with the rest of the sample code in this chapter, head to our companion website and download the data file `favourites-survey.csv` onto your computer. Take note of where you save it to as you'll have to place it in the same folder as your Python code (`.py` file) to make it available.

> The data file we will be using is saved using a format called *comma-separated values* (csv), where each piece of data is separated using a comma, and each entry is in its own line. Maintaining this format is important as this will be how the chatbots extract and interpret the data.

```
Timestamp,"Who are you? (Please provide a distinctive, memorable *fake* name)",Wha
pet?,Favourite world cuisine?,Favourite hobby?,What career did you think you'd hav
study?,Whose section are you in?
9-30-2020 9:36:24,Zephyr,Comedy,Dog,Japanese,Playing video games,Architect,Morning
9-30-2020 9:45:35,Brain,Horror,Dog,Japanese,Playing video games,engineer,Evening,V
9-30-2020 9:46:12,Victoria,Comedy,Cat,Italian,Playing video games,Teacher,Afternoo
9-30-2020 10:04:13,Yovarn,Action,Dog,Japanese,Other,Teacher,Evening,Harinder Khang
9-30-2020 10:17:54,Clive Donnovan,Comedy,Bird,Japanese,Working out,Celebrity,Eveni
9-30-2020 10:33:29,John Wood,Action,Dog,Japanese,Playing video games,I never thoug
9-30-2020 10:33:32,Dana,Action,Dog,Japanese,Painting or drawing,Doctor,Late night,
9-30-2020 10:33:36,Thick,Animated,Dog,Chinese,Playing video games,Train Conductor,
9-30-2020 10:33:41,Sarah Ho,Drama,Dog,Chinese,Playing video games,Cjef,Morning,Har
9-30-2020 10:33:43,Charles Xavier,Sci-fi,Dog,Thai,Playing video games,Writer,Eveni
9-30-2020 10:33:48,Theo Von,Comedy,Dog,Japanese,Playing a sport,Athlete,Evening,Ha
9-30-2020 10:33:53,I LOVE U,Comedy,Dog,Malaysian,Playing video games,Teacher,After
```

Figure 3.7 The content in a plain text file. Both human and computers can read it.

This data file contains the results of a survey sent to a group of students. The survey asked the students about their preferences in movies, pets, time of study, and other information.

3.2.3   Favourite Pets

We have run a survey online and extracted the data into a file. Let's write a chatbot that looks into the data file and finds out whether there are more respondents who like cats as pets or who like dogs as pets. We are going to use code similar to that for the Popular Cafe Finder bot to tally up votes for cats and dogs (you can also use a dictionary as illustrated in the Movie Rater bot example above).

Let's begin with exploring the contents of our file. First, use the open function to create a reference to the file (line 7). Next, we call a method of this reference (readline ()) to read the first line, or header, of the file (it's useful for humans to know the meaning of the comma-separated values, but the chatbot doesn't need this line to tally up the votes). We call the readline() function again, and it captures the next line in the file.

```
1   # Favourite Pets Bot
2   # Author:
3   # Date:
4   # Find out whether the survey-takers like cats
5   # or dogs more
6
7   file = open("favourites-survey.csv")
8
9   # Get the header information
10  header = file.readline()
11  print(header)
12
13  # Get the first line of data
14  data = file.readline()
15  print(data)
```

The code and the data file must be in the same folder on your computer (or in your online environment) for the code to work. This is because the program is only going to look for the data file in the same folder as the code. If you see the `FileNotFoundError`, make sure that this is the case.

If we print the values of the variables containing the result of the `readline()` function, we obtain the following output.

```
"Timestamp","Who are you? (Please provide a distinctive, memorable *
fake* name)","What is your favourite movie genre?","Favourite animal
 as a pet?","Favourite world cuisine?","Favourite hobby?","What care
er did you think you'd have as a kid?","What time of the day do you
prefer to study?"

"2021/02/03 11:06:01 AM PST","Jayrad","Comedy","Dog","Italian","Lear
ning new languages","Teacher","Morning"
```

Figure 3.8 The first two lines of the `favourites-survey.csv` file.

Now, we need to process the contents of the data variable, which is of string type. One way to do this is to convert the string into a list. We can use the `split()` function, which allows us to split the string into a list, based on a separation character of our choice. In the code below, we instruct our program to split on the comma character.

```
1   # Favourite Pets Bot
2   # Author:
3   # Date:
4   # Find out whether the survey-takers like cats
5   # or dogs more
6
7   file = open("favourites-survey.csv")
8
9   # Get the header information
10  header = file.readline()
11  print(header)
12
13  # Get the first line of data
14  data = file.readline()
15  print(data)
16
17  # Split the data into a list
18  datalist = data.strip().split(",")
19  print(datalist)
```

We can see the output of our latest program below.

Figure 3.9 The first two lines of the file, plus the list corresponding to the first line of data.

This list representation of our data is extremely useful, because we can access each piece of data individually using *indexing*. Indexing allows us to specify which element in the list we wish to access. The first element is at index 0, the second element is at index 1, and so on.

```
1   # Favourite Pets Bot
2   # Author:
3   # Date:
4   # Find out whether the survey-takers like cats
5   # or dogs more
6
7   file = open("favourites-survey.csv")
8
9   # Get the header information
10  header = file.readline()
11  print(header)
12
13  # Get the first line of data
14  data = file.readline()
15  print(data)
16
17  # Split the data into a list
18  datalist = data.strip().split(",")
19  print(datalist)
20
21  # Access the 3rd element, at index 2
22  print(datalist[2])
```

Try it! The program should now additionally print out Comedy, which is the element at index 2. Note: It is important to remember that list indexing begins at 0, not 1! Generally, computer scientists like counting from 0! How would you access the value corresponding to Dog?

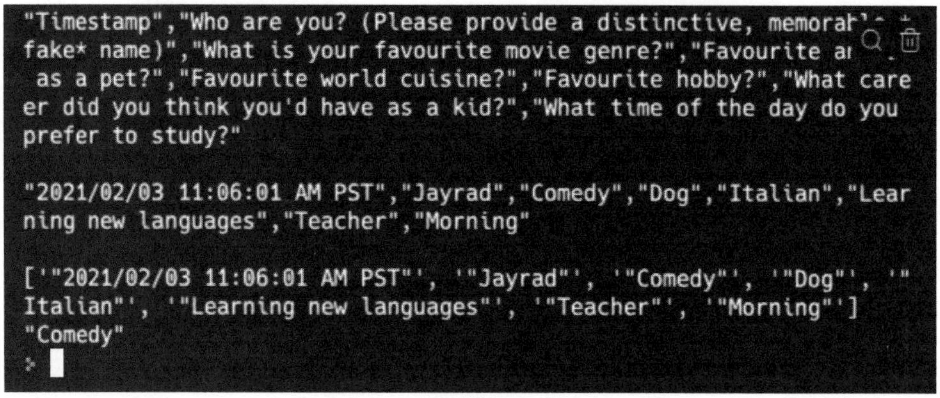

Figure 3.10 The first two lines of the file, plus the list corresponding to the first line of data, and finally the element at index 2.

Now that we have understood how to access an element of list using its **index**, we can see how we might access each line in the file. The following program uses a `for`-loop paradigm to access each line, without needing to call `readline()` each time. We add a few other features, described below.

```
1   # Favourite Pets Bot
2   # Author:
3   # Date:
4   # Find out whether the survey-takers like cats
5   # or dogs more
6
7   # Open the file
8   file = open("favourites-survey.csv")
9
10  # Get the header information
11  header = file.readline()
12
13  # Initialize tallies
14  cat_tally = 0
15  dog_tally = 0
16
17  for line in file:
18
19      # Split the data into a list
20      datalist = line.strip().split(",")
21
22      # Access the element of the list
23      # corresponding to pet
24      pet = datalist[3]
25
26      if "Cat" in pet:
27          cat_tally += 1
28      elif "Dog" in pet:
```

```
29      dog_tally += 1
30
31  # Prints out tallies for cat and dog
32  print("Cat people:",cat_tally)
33  print("Dog people:",dog_tally)
```

Lines 17–29 represent a for-loop programming construct that goes through the data file line by line. Each time the loop repeats, the following happens:

- one line from the data file is read into the program and is made available through the variable line as a string
- the method split(",") is called in the method chain to divide up the line into a list of strings at places where a comma appears
- the method strip() is called to remove leading and trailing characters of the line (including return carriages), which csv files use to maintain their structure but can result in errors when using split
- the fourth (not third, as list index starts a 0) item in the list, which is the type of pet, is accessed and stored in the pet string variable

Finally, depending on the results of the survey data file, the if-elif conditional programming construct adds a vote to the corresponding tally, and we can summarize the results.

```
1   # Favourite Pets Bot
2   # Author:
3   # Date:
4   # Find out whether the survey-takers like cats
5   # or dogs more
6
7   # Open the file
8   file = open("favourites-survey.csv")
9
10  # Get the header information
11  header = file.readline()
12
13  # Initialize tallies
14  cat_tally = 0
15  dog_tally = 0
16
17  for line in file:
18
19      # Split the data into a list
20      datalist = line.strip().split(",")
21
22      # Access the element of the list
23      # corresponding to pet
24      pet = datalist[3]
25
26      if "Cat" in pet:
```

```
27        cat_tally += 1
28    elif "Dog" in pet:
29        dog_tally += 1
30
31  # Prints out tallies for cat and dog
32  print("Cat people:",cat_tally)
33  print("Dog people:",dog_tally)
34
35  # Using comparison operators, make a
36  # statement about the cat vs. dog results
37  if cat_tally < dog_tally:
38    print("Dog lovers win!")
39  elif cat_tally > dog_tally:
40    print("There are more cat people in the class!")
41  elif cat_tally == dog_tally:
42    print("It's a tie!")
43
44  # A few other things you could say
45  if cat_tally < 1:
46    print("No one is a cat person!")
47  elif 50 < cat_tally and cat_tally < dog_tally:
48    print("Lots of cat people, but not as many as dogs!")
```

By the time this for-loop finishes (it ends automatically if there are no more lines in the file to read), the chatbot will have gone through the entire data file and tallied up the votes for cats and dogs (ignoring other pets). Then it is just a matter of how to report the findings.

WRITING TO A FILE

Now that we've learned how to open and process a file, we can also place the contents of our report into a new file to save it to our computer. To do this, use the open() method to open a file, but add an argument w, which stands for "write," like this: outfile=open ("favourites-report.txt","w"). This creates a new text file called favourites -report.txt that you can write to, or, if it is already there, opens an existing file for writing. Try this out by adding the following code snippet at the end of your previous program.

```
49  outfile = open("favourites-report.csv","w")
50  outfile.write("Pet\tTally\n")
51  outfile.write("Cats"+"\t"+str(cat_tally)+"\n")
52  outfile.write("Dogs"+"\t"+str(dog_tally)+"\n")
53  file.close()
54  outfile.close()
```

Notice that you use write() to write to the file, and that at the end of the line you add a \n, which indicates a newline. We also place a tab between each of our data elements using \t. In addition, notice that you need to convert your integer variables cat_tally and dog_tally into strings by using the `str()` function. Finally, it is best practice to close all the files you have opened, using the `close()` method.

Once you run this code, you will find that a new file has been created in the same folder as your Python file. If it exists already, it will be overwritten, so proceed with caution as Python will not warn you that you are overwriting an existing file!

> Challenge: Try to create a report that tallies up the votes for all the pet types. Use the parallel lists technique from Sec. 3.1.4 given a list of pets such as Dog, Cat, Turtle, Fish, Rat, and Bird and a list of their respective tallies that you create. Then output a report with the number of votes for each pet type. For an extra challenge, report which pet type has the largest number of votes!

3.2.4 Similarity Score

One way that recommendation systems work is to find people who are similar to each other, i.e., have similar tastes and preferences.

For example, if Alice likes bananas, cherries, and apples, and Bob likes bananas, cherries, and durians, we might say that Alice and Bob are similar: they have two common favourite fruits. We could also guess that, perhaps, Alice might like durians, and Bob might like apples.

How might you quantify the extent to which two persons are similar? One way to find out is to ask them about their preferences and count the number of common answers. For instance, say Charlie likes oranges, pineapples, and bananas. Then Alice is more similar to Bob than to Charlie, as Alice and Bob have two common fruits they like (bananas and cherries); whereas there is only one common fruit between Alice and Charlie (bananas).

Let's write a small program that counts the number of common favourite movies between two people:

```
1  # Comparing two person's favourite movies
2  # Author:
3  # Date:
4  # Description: Finds out how similar two persons
5  # are by comparing their favourite movies lists
6
7  # Get the favourite movies for each person
8  angelica_favourite_movies = ["Big Hero 6",
9                               "Inside Out",
10                              "Wall-E"]
11 victor_favourite_movies = ["Big Hero 6",
12                            "Star Wars",
13                            "Wall-E"]
14
15 # Initialize a common interests counter
16 common_interests_counter = 0
17
```

```
18   # Go through all the favourite movies
19   # of the first person
20   for movie in angelica_favourite_movies:
21
22      # Is that movie also in the 2nd person's list?
23      if movie in victor_favourite_movies:
24
25         # Add to the common interests counter
26         common_interests_counter += 1
27
28   # Print the result
29   print(common_interests_counter)
```

As you can see, the more the number of common answers two persons have, the higher the similarity score will be.

This small program, together with the above tallying examples (and the Favourite Cafe program), also demonstrates a very useful computation technique called **accumulator pattern**: we create a few counter variables and set them to an initial value. When we go through the data and see something worth noting, we update the corresponding counter variable by adding 1 to it. After all the data is examined, we can look at a summary of how many times something worth noting has occurred. In other words, we *accumulate* information as we examine the data.

A variation of this accumulator pattern is one in which, instead of incrementing the counter variable, we update a variable to the value of some information we find worth recording. You will see an example in the next section.

3.2.5   Who Is Most Similar to You?

Combining what we have covered from the previous three sections (reading data files, tallying systems, and calculating similarity scores), we have everything we need to write a chatbot that provides recommendations based on similarity!

The goal of this recommendation chatbot is to find the person who is most similar to you, that is, having the most number of common interests as you.

To start, modify the csv file by adding to the second line (just below the header line) a line indicating your preferences. For example:

```
2022/01/01 0:00:00 AM MDT,John Smith,Action,Dog,Italian,Playing
video games,Dentist,Afternoon
```

The first item is a timestamp, which the chatbot won't be using, so you can write any time there. For the rest, you can refer to the data file to get some inspiration. Make sure you have the same number of items (eight) an all the lines. Save the file and close it when you are done.

Then write the following code:

```
1   # Most Similar Person Finder
2   # Author:
3   # Date:
4   # Description: Find the person with the largest
5   # similarity score
```

```
 6
 7   # Open the file
 8   # Remove/process header
 9   file = open("favourites-survey.csv")
10   header = file.readline()
11
12   # Read the first line of data
13   # representing my preferences
14   my_favourites = file.readline()\
15                       .strip()\
16                       .split(",")[2:]
17   print(my_favourites)
18
19   # Initialize variables for top friend (no one)
20   # and top score (0)
21   top_friend = ""
22   top_score = 0
23
24   # Go through each line of the file
25   for person in file:
26
27     # Get their favourites
28     person_data = person.strip().split(",")
29     # All the elements after the person's name
30     person_favourites = person_data[2:]
31     person_name = person_data[1]
32
33     # Get similarity score
34     common_interest_tally = 0
35     # For each of my favourite things
36     # check if it's also in theirs
37     for favourite in my_favourites:
38       if favourite in person_favourites:
39         common_interest_tally += 1
40
41     # Check if their score is higher than
42     # the current top score
43     if common_interest_tally > top_score:
44       # If so, set the top friend name to them
45       top_friend = person_name
46       # and update the top score
47       top_score = common_interest_tally
48
49   # Print the top friend
50   print(top_friend, top_score)
```

You might have noticed when preparing the list of interests that the code adds a [2:] at the end of the chained method calls (lines 16 and 30). This small piece of code is called **list slicing** where by Python creates a "slice" of the original list using the content in the

[and]. The 2: means a slice starting from the index 2 and including the rest of the items. We create this slice so that we can create a list containing only the favourite items, cropping out the timestamp and name. You can choose to create a smaller slice by playing with the values (left as an exercise here).

This code is an example of a variation of the **accumulator pattern** explained in the previous section. In fact, what we are calculating now is not a tally, but the **maximum value** in the list. Here, we initialize a variable (top_score) with the lowest possible value. As the program goes through the data file, it calculates different similarity scores (common_interest_tally). When it finds one that is larger than the current value stored in top_score, it updates top_score with the larger value (line 47). Then, after all the lines are examined, top_score will store the largest value that has appeared during the examination. To help the program to remember which person has resulted in the largest value, we create a separate variable top_friend, which gets updated (line 45) with the corresponding person's name when top_score is updated.

We can further apply this pattern to the chatbot to improve the recommendations it provides. Right now it can only tell us one person who has the highest similarity score. What if we think those who have a similarity score over 2 should also be part of the recommendations? Using an additional accumulator variable that accumulates the names of multiple persons, the chatbot will be able to recommend all who have a similarity score over 2.

Modify the above code as follows:

- add an additional accumulator variable called top_friends below the other accumulator variables and initialize it as an empty list [ ]
- add an if-statement programming construct as the last code segment in the for-loop (below and at the same indentation level as the code segment checking whether the similarity score is higher than the current top score. If the similarity score is above 2, use this statement to accumulate the person's name to the accumulator variable: top_friends += [person_name] Indeed, we can concatenate lists, in the same way that we can concatenate strings!

Now our recommendation chatbot is complete! Try replacing your preferences with your friends' preferences and see if they get the same recommendations!

3.2.6   Review Questions

Time to test how much you understand the content in this chapter. It is okay to go back and review!

THEORY AND UNDERSTANDING

- How would you open a file called survey.txt?
- How would you access the second to last element in a list called favourites?
- What are two ways to read a line from a file?
- How would you split a string of words into a list? Imagine that the words are separated by ;
- A list contains the following:

```
1   singers = ["elle", "anne", "snowman"]
```

Who is in singers[2]?

• What would this code output?

```
1  response = "I LOVE COFFEE!!"
2  words = response.lower().strip("!").split(" ")
3  if "coffee" in words or "starbucks" in words:
4      print("Caffeine junkie, eh?")
5  else:
6      print("Hmm...")
```

• What does the following code output?

```
1  pets = "cats, dogs, birds"
2  petlist = pets.split(",")
3  print("cats" in petlist)
4  print("dogs" in petlist)
```

• What does this output?

```
1  foods = ["cherries", "tomatoes"]
2  print(foods[1][0].upper())
```

SYNTAX SELF-CHECK

What do the following functions and keywords mean?

• `file = open("myfile.txt")`
• `file.readline()`
• `for line in file:`
• `mystring.split(...)`
• `mystring.strip(...)`
• `mystring[0]`
• `mystring[-1]`
• `mystring[:]`
• `mystring[3:5]`
• `mystring[:3]`
• `mystring[3:]`
• `"a"*3`
• `["a"]*3`
• `alist[2][0]`
• `list1+list2`
• `list1 = list1 + [elem]`
• `alist[0]`
• `alist[:3]`
• `alist[1:3]`
• `alist[4:4]`
• `alist[4:]`
• `alist[3:-1]`
• `"a"<"b"`

3.2.7 Practice Exercises

CODING

Now it's time for you to practice by writing some code. When you are done, you can go to the Solutions section on our companion website to compare your answers with ours. Note that there can be many answers to the same question, so don't worry if yours are not the same as ours. The important things are that they produce the same results, and you are able to tell where the differences are and why both answers work.

SIMILAR HOBBY FINDER

Write a program that calculates the similarity score (defined as the number of common interests) between two person's hobbies. The program should take as input two strings with hobbies separated with spaces. It should be robust to uppercases/lowercases and different orders. For example, "Skiing Drawing coding" and "Knitting skating Coding" should output a similarity score of 1.

Here are two sample runs:

```
Please enter hobbies, separated by spaces.
Person 1: skiing drawing climbing
Person 2: drawing skiing singing
You have 2 hobbies in common!
>
```

```
Please enter hobbies, separated by spaces.
Person 1: Snowboarding TV Coding
Person 2: coding tv snowboarding
You have 3 hobbies in common!
>
```

Figure 3.11 The case where there are two hobbies in common.

Figure 3.12 The case where there are three hobbies in common.

PARENT BOT

Write a program that asks four questions. Every time you say yes, your points increase. The questions are:

*   Did you eat?
*   Did you study?
*   Did you do your laundry?
*   Did you call grandma?

At the end, the program will reply to you as follows:

*   0 points: `I'm coming over`
*   1–2 points: `Ok.`
*   3–4 points: `Good!`

Your code should use a loop to ask the questions and use at least one of these comparison operators (`<`, `>`, `<=`, `>=`, `==`). It should also use the accumulator pattern to tally the number of `yes`s.

```
Did you eat? no
Did you study? no
Did you do your laundry? no
Did you call grandma? no
I'm coming over.
>
```

```
Did you eat? yes
Did you study? yes
Did you do your laundry? yes
Did you call grandma? yes
Good!
>
```

```
Did you eat? yes
Did you study? no
Did you do your laundry? yes
Did you call grandma? umm
Ok.
>
```

Figure 3.13 Parent is coming over.

Figure 3.14 The kid is behaving.

Figure 3.15 The kid could do better.

3.2.8   Glossary

- **CSV files**, human-readable text files in which pieces of data are separated by commas (comma-separated values), and each entry is in its own line. Some productivity applications (e.g., Microsoft Excel) automatically convert these files into tables, but you can always open them with a normal text editor to see the values and even modify them.
- **header line**, the first line in a data file indicating what the values in the subsequent lines of the file represent. Typically when a program retrieves data from the data file, this line will be ignored as it does not contain any value (some data files does not even have this line). But it is very useful for the user to make sense of the data when the program is displaying the data.
- **accumulator pattern**, a computational technique to aggregate information as the program goes through the data. This technique involves setting up a counter/accumulator variable and assigning an initial value to it. As the program examines the data, this variable gets updated according to some rules. An example is that of counting the number of even numbers in a data file: set up a counter variable with an initial value 0, as the program examines the values, increment this counter variable by 1 each time it sees an even number. When all the values are examined, the counter variable holds the number of even numbers. The same technique can be used to analyze all values in the data file in other ways, for example, to calculate the total of all values (keep adding to the variable), and to find the largest value (update the variable when a larger value appears).
- **list slicing**, a functionality in Python to extract a portion of a list. Instead of using an index to access an item in the list, one can use numbers and a colon to specify which portion to extract. For example, 3:5 means the portion starting from the index 3 to the index 4 (= 5 − 1). If one of the numbers is missing, it means all the items on that side are to be extracted. For example, :5 means the portion from the index 0 to the index 4; and 3: means the portion from the index 3 to the last index of the list.

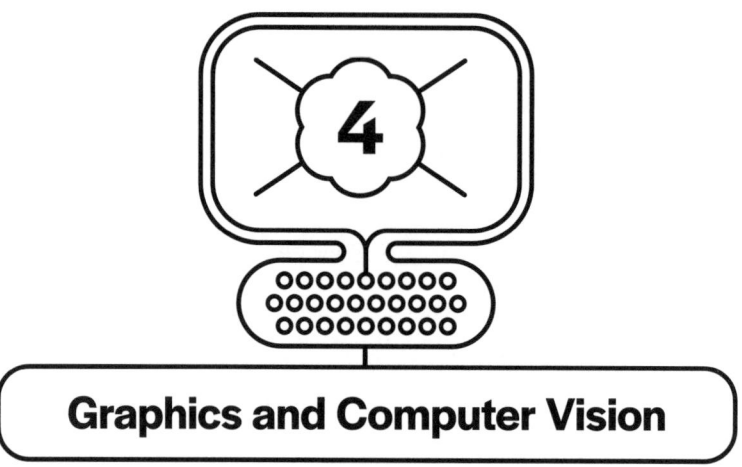

Graphics and Computer Vision

One big use of computers is to both process and generate graphics and images. In this chapter you'll learn how computers do that and use them to create something nice!

Animated movies and video games today rely heavily on 2D and 3D graphics and animation technology to generate realistic-looking, high-resolution content. At the end of the day, the process is about figuring out what colour to use in each pixel. In many cases, computers are provided with instructions for making that decision: for example, what a colour should be given multiple light sources, and how many times something needs to be drawn over and over again. Here, we'll show you how you can use Python to create simple drawings and manipulate images, which is fundamental to more advanced computer vision and graphics algorithms.

> **FUN FACT:** There is a frame in the Disney movie *Frozen* that took more than 132 hours to render (that's more than five days)! Talk about computers being frozen.

The chatbot programs that you'll be writing include:

- Interactive Drawing with `turtle`
- Cookie Drawer
- Input Validator
- Number Guessing Game
- Green Screen Magic Bot

Through writing these chatbot programs in Python, you'll learn about ways to store and access sophisticated data, create functions, use packages/modules, and draw things. You will also learn about some concepts in computer graphics.

CS topics in this unit:

- `turtle` module
- `while`-loop
- Functions
- Parameters

- Recursion
- Fruitful functions
- Selective import
- 2D arrays
- RGB representations
- Modules
- Problem solving strategies
- Nested loops

4.1   INTERACTIVE DRAWINGS

Many of the animated movies you see nowadays consist of many frames of images generated by code. Some of this code is quite simple. Yet, when you combine them with some programming constructs, they generate intricate drawings that you can manipulate and even incorporate some randomness into.

In this section we introduce Python `turtle`, a Python module that creates drawings based on commands. We begin with some basic commands, and then discuss how to draw intricate patterns and shapes by combining them in an efficient way.

4.1.1   Learning Outcomes

At the end of this unit, you will be able to ...

THE TURTLE MODULE

- use the `turtle` module to create drawings
- read and understand basic `turtle` code to visualize its output
- color the turtle using `turtle` color names as well as RGB color values coded as 3-tuples

DEFINING FUNCTIONS

- create a function with and without parameters
- call a function previously created in the program
- call a function from a loop, possibly using the loop index as part of the arguments
- identify the scope of a variable, especially in relation to a function's scope

4.1.2   Basic `Turtle` Commands

The main idea of Python `turtle` is to give you full control of a "turtle" that moves around leaving trails. The trails are part of the drawing that you can modify by changing their color or appearance.

The first thing you want to do is import the `turtle` module so you have access to its definitions and commands. Then, you can create a turtle and give it a name by which you can refer to it in the rest of your code.

```
1   # Basic Turtle Commands
2   # Author:
3   # Date:
4   # Description: Quick demo of some of the basic
```

```
 5  # Turtle commands
 6
 7  import turtle
 8
 9  fred = turtle.Turtle()
10
11  fred.forward(100)
12  fred.stamp()
13  fred.penup()
14  fred.forward(100)
15  fred.pendown()
16  fred.stamp()
```

Here are some of the motion/state commands that our turtle `fred` accepts:

- `forward(distance)`—move forward by the specified distance, in the direction the turtle is headed (where the pointy bit is pointing at).
- `right(units)`—turn the turtle right by the specified units. By default they are in degrees.
- `left(units)`—turn the turtle left by the specified units. By default they are in degrees.
- `circle(radius)`—draw a circle with the specified radius. The center is `radius` units above the turtle. You can include a few more controls on how the circle is drawn by providing some extra arguments.
- `stamp`—stamp a copy of the turtle shape onto the canvas at the current turtle position. You can change the shape of the turtle using the `shape` command.
- `penup`—pull the pen up so that no trail is left when moving.
- `pendown`—put the pen down so that a trail is left when moving.

Give them a try, modify the code and see how different your drawings are from those in the demo.

For more commands supported by the turtle, refer to https://docs.python.org/3/library/turtle.html.

4.1.3   Interactive Drawing with Turtle

Let's create an interactive chatbot that lets the user issue commands to draw in real time via the turtle it controls.

To start, this chatbot will only draw a short line in the direction the turtle is facing. But the user can control how many times it draws the line.

```
1  # Interactive Drawing with Turtle
2  # Author:
3  # Date:
4  # The turtle will take commands to move and draw
5  # It will keep asking for a command until
6  # you say stop
7  # f: forward 10 pixels
8  # s: stamp
```

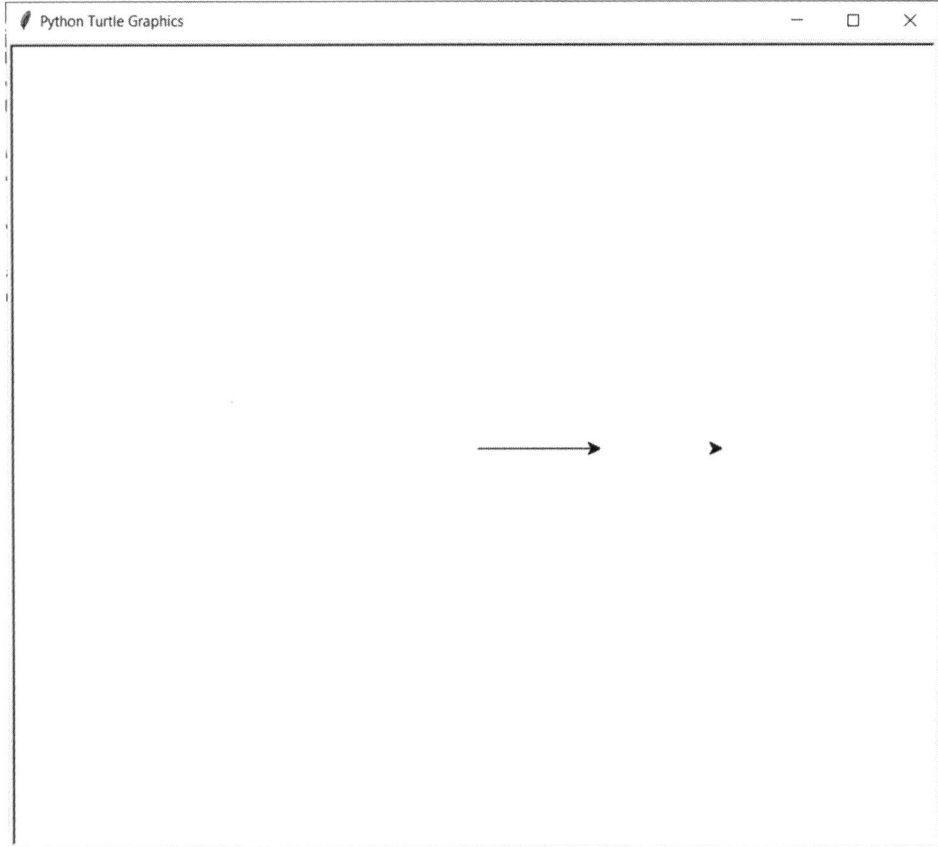

Figure 4.1 Quick demo of some of the basic `turtle` commands.

```
 9  # stop: exit the loop
10
11  # Create a turtle
12  import turtle
13
14  anna = turtle.Turtle()
15
16  # Create a boolean sentinel/flag
17  keep_looping = True
18
19  while keep_looping:
20      # Ask what the user wants to do
21      command = input("What would you like me to do?").lower()
22
23      # If the user types s, stamp
24      if command == "s":
25          anna.stamp()
26      # If the user types f, go forward
27      elif command == "f":
```

```
28        anna.forward(10)
29    elif command == "stop":
30        keep_looping = False
```

This chatbot is rather simple, isn't it? Try including a few more commands, for example, l to turn left by 90 degrees, r to turn right by 90 degrees.

When we first built our chatbots in the previous chapters, we didn't have a way for the bot to ask again whether it didn't receive an acceptable response, or to end only if a certain response was received.

In the code above we use a new programming construct, the while-loop, to enable that. Similar to a for-loop, the while-loop repeats the code inside; but instead of using a list to control how many times it repeats, it uses a Boolean sentinel/flag to determine if it is going to repeat.

In line 17 we create a Boolean variable called **keep_looping**, which stores the initial value True. When the while-loop begins the first time, it checks whether the variable's value is True or False. If the value is True, it executes the code inside; if not, it skips the code and never repeats itself. After each repetition, the while-loop will check the variable's value again and decide whether it is going to repeat or skip. It is therefore very important to have some code inside the while-loop to update the value of the sentinel/flag variable so that the loop will eventually end (line 30).

This use of a Boolean variable as a sentinel/flag alongside a while-loop is a very common technique for input validation. Imagine the Boolean variable is the result of a validity check of an input string (e.g., does it have a number inside? is it long enough?). You can use the Boolean variable to store the answer to the question: is the input string invalid? If so, it will be True and the while-loop will repeat; otherwise it will be False and the while-loop will end. Try to write this code!

4.1.4   Cookie Drawer

Now let's draw something a bit more intricate, for example, a cookie with some chocolate chips on top!

```
1    import turtle
2
3    fred = turtle.Turtle()
4
5    fred.circle(30)
6    fred.penup()
7    fred.goto(5, 30) #where the middle chip is
8    fred.stamp()
9    for x in [-5, 15]:
10       fred.goto(x, 20)
```

```
11      fred.stamp()
12      fred.goto(x, 40)
13      fred.stamp();
```

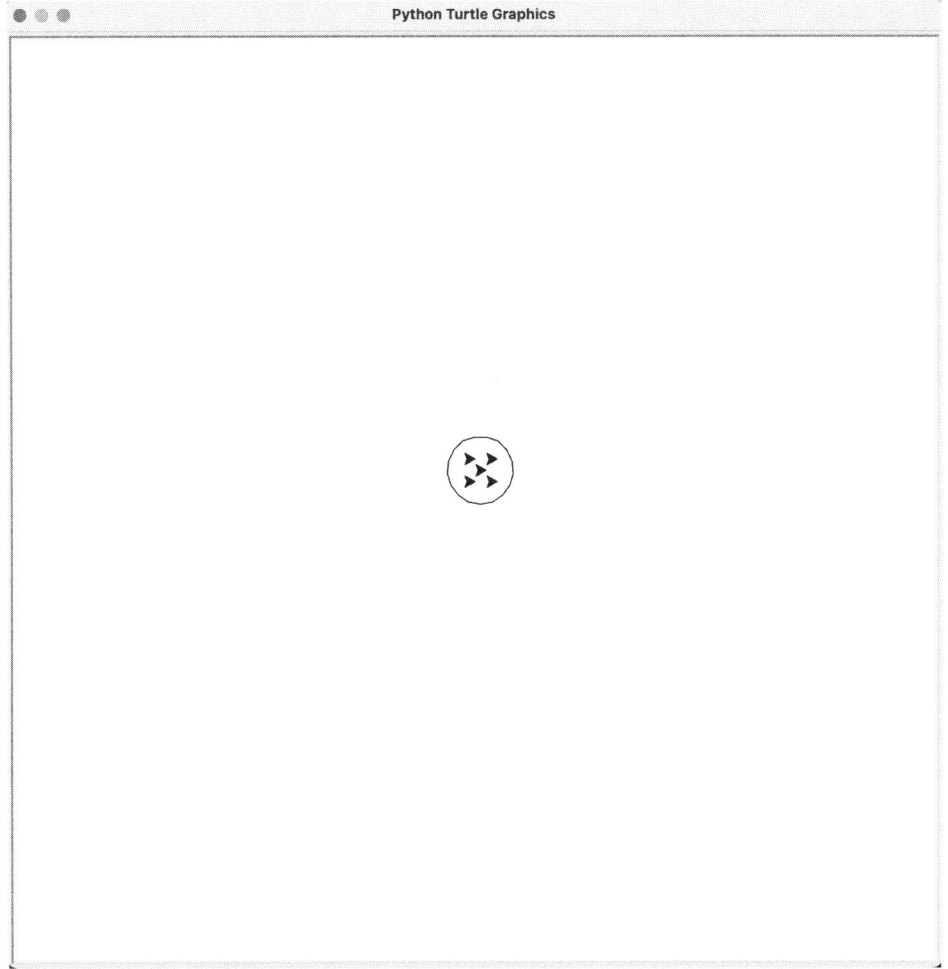

Figure 4.2 One chocolate chip cookie!

The above code snippet draws one cookie by drawing a circle and then some chocolate chips using the `stamp()` method. It uses the method `goto`, which moves the turtle to the position specified by the arguments. We use the `penup()` method (line 6) so that when the turtle moves to the specified location it doesn't leave a trail (as if it jumps there). We also use a `for`-loop to shorten the code so that a pair of chocolate chips is drawn for each loop iteration.

`turtle` uses a two-dimensional coordinate system to manage its position. The first value is the x-position (horizontal), which becomes negative as you go left and positive as you go right. The second value is the y-position (vertical), which

> becomes negative as you go down and positive as you go up. The middle of the canvas has the position (0, 0), which is also called **home**, and you can go there by calling the home() method.

This looks great. But what if we want to draw a few more cookies? Do we need to copy this code multiple times? We can certainly do that, but this will make our code much longer. Also, if we want to change how the cookie looks (e.g., a bigger cookie with more chocolate chips), we will have to go to all of the copies and make the change.

In programming we have a construct that allows us to reuse the code after it is written, with a bit of flexibility on how the code is being reused. This programming construct is called a **function**. In fact, you have seen it many times in our code samples! For example, print() is a function that we reuse many times to print something to the display, and it is flexible enough so that we can make it print different things. Another example is the random.choice() method, which randomly picks an item from the list we provide it with.

> As explained previously, we have been using both "functions" and "methods" to refer to bits of code that we can reuse. The distinction is whether it is a code associated to a variable/object: if it isn't we call it function; otherwise we call it method. Since choice() is associated to the random object, we call it a method of the random object.

The process of creating this reusable function programming construct is called "defining a function." First, we use the def keyword to indicate that we are defining a function. Then, we decide on a name for the function and what information it needs when it is being reused. Finally, we put the code it executes in the *function body*. For example, below is a function that draws one cookie.

```
1   def drawOneCookie(x_offset, y_offset):
2       # goto the starting position
3       fred.penup()
4       fred.goto(x_offset, y_offset)
5       fred.pendown()
6
7       fred.circle(30)
8       fred.penup()
9       fred.goto(5+x_offset, 30+y_offset)
10      fred.stamp()
11      for x in [-5, 15]:
12          fred.goto(x+x_offset, 20+y_offset)
13          fred.stamp()
14          fred.goto(x+x_offset, 40+y_offset)
15          fred.stamp();
```

This function uses two parameters, x_offset and y_offset, to move the turtle to the desired position on the canvas to draw. This is how the function becomes flexible in drawing one cookie at different positions.

If you write the code from the previous page (after the importing and after creating a turtle) and run the code, you will notice that nothing gets drawn. The reason is this code is just a definition, and Python will not execute it unless you "call" it.

To call a function, you are going to use its name, and provide all the necessary information (as arguments) for it to know exactly what to do. For our function, the name is drawOneCookie, and the information will be where it starts drawing the cookie.

Here is the complete code where the function is called three times to draw three cookies:

```
1   import turtle
2
3   fred = turtle.Turtle()
4
5   def drawOneCookie(x_offset, y_offset):
6       # goto the starting position
7       fred.penup()
8       fred.goto(x_offset, y_offset)
9       fred.pendown()
10
11      fred.circle(30)
12      fred.penup()
13      fred.goto(5+x_offset, 30+y_offset)
14      fred.stamp()
15      for x in [-5, 15]:
16          fred.goto(x+x_offset, 20+y_offset)
17          fred.stamp()
18          fred.goto(x+x_offset, 40+y_offset)
19          fred.stamp();
20
21  drawOneCookie(-100, 0)
22  drawOneCookie(50, 50)
23  drawOneCookie(100, 20)
```

Check out Figure 4.3 to see how our multi-cookie drawing looks!
Yum! Try drawing a few more cookies!

4.1.5   Review Questions

Time to test how much you understand the content in this chapter. It is okay to go back and review!

THEORY AND UNDERSTANDING
- What is the benefit of defining a function?
- What is the keyword necessary to create a function?
- What are function parameters good for?
- How do we create a turtle object, given the turtle module?

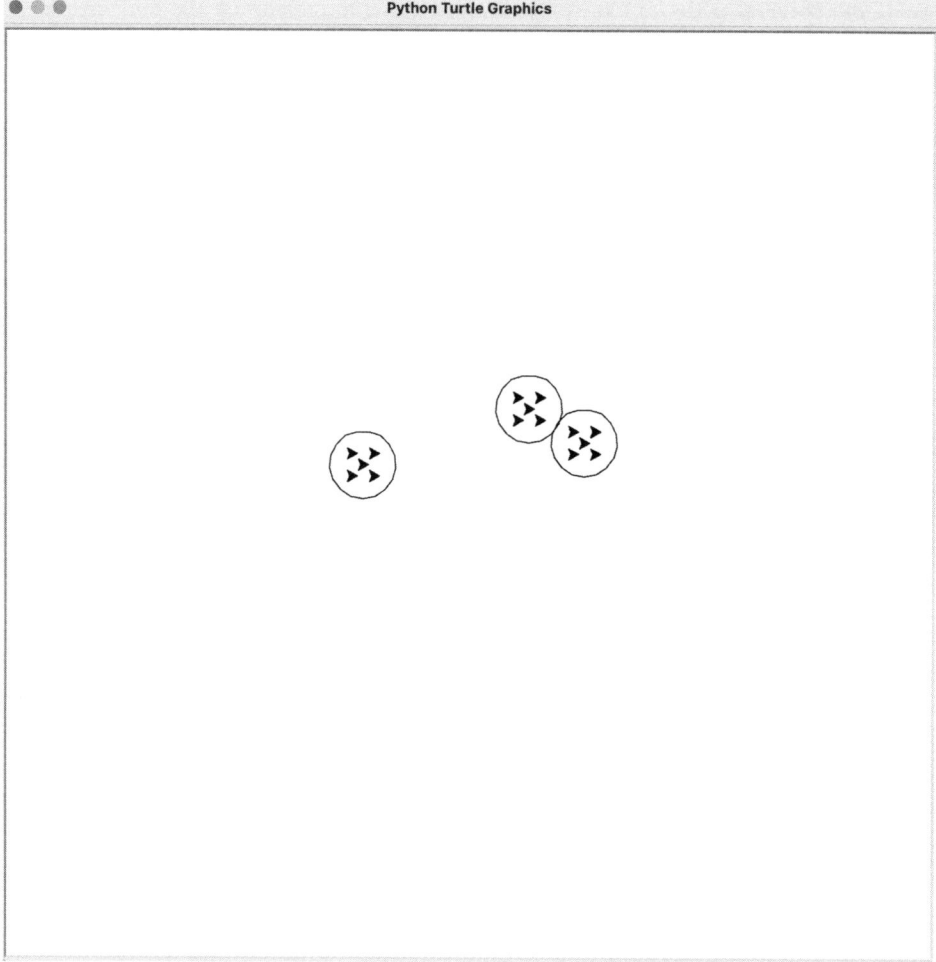

Figure 4.3 Drawing three cookies using a function.

SYNTAX SELF-CHECK

What do the functions and keywords in the following code snippets mean?

- Snippet 1:

```
1     import turtle
2     pet = turtle.Turtle()
3     pet.forward(10)
4     pet.stamp()
5     pet.right(180)
6     pet.left(90)
7     pet.penup()
8     pet.pendown()
9     pet.goto(10,-10)
10    pet.color("blue")
```

- Snippet 2:

```
1    turtle.colormode(255)
2    mycolor = (255,0,120)
3    pet.color(mycolor)
```

- Snippet 3:

```
1    adam = turtle.Turtle()
2    def myfunction(a,b):
3        adam.goto(a, b)
4        adam.stamp()
5    for i in range(5):
6        myfunction(i*20, i)
```

4.2   IMAGE PROCESSING

Another common functionality we use computers for is processing images. Think about the times when you applied a filter to a photo you took, or cropped/resized it to a size you liked. In the movie industry, computers are also used to process frames (images) by removing unwanted artifacts and replacing backgrounds.

In this section, we will explain how basic image processing works, and you'll write Python code to process and understand images. To start, we need to import a Python package called pygame, which includes several modules to process and manipulate images. This package might not be installed on your computer. To test if it is installed, simply type this import statement:

    import pygame

and run your code. If Python gives you an error saying that the package is missing, you will have to install it before you can proceed.

> In the coding environments listed in Section 1.1.3, Trinket and Mu both have pygame preinstalled. If you are using other environments, you might have to install pygame yourself. For details about how to install pygame, refer to https://www.pygame.org.

4.2.1   Learning Outcomes

At the end of this unit, you will be able to …

DEFINING FRUITFUL/PRODUCTIVE FUNCTIONS

- create and use functions that return values
- call a function so that the value returned from a function is received
- state the effect that a return has if executed inside a loop (inside a function)
- identify cases when the value None is produced when calling a function
- use modules containing one's own defined functions (import and use a short name)

THE WHILE-LOOP

- identify when a `while`-loop would be appropriate compared to a `for`-loop
- create a valid `while`-loop with a sentinel (control variable), and with multiple control variables
- use a `while`-loop to validate user input

IMAGE PROCESSING

- how pixel colors are represented by RGB values
- access and modify a 2D image in the form of a list of lists, containing RGB values in the form of a list (a 3D list)
- extract and/or change the color as RGB and/or individual color components of a pixel in a 3D list

LISTS

- know what a list alias is, versus a copy
- know the implication of sending a list as an argument to a function (it becomes an alias)
- know how to modify a list using `append()`
- know the effect of modifying a list inside a function when the list is sent as an argument, even if it is not returned

4.2.2   Green or Not?

Did you know that some of your favourite movie action sequences are filmed in front of a green screen? After filming, special effects studios use computer software to separate people and objects from the background, which is then replaced with something else (e.g., a space background). One easy way to do this is to assume that the background is of a specific colour, such as bright green. When the computer program senses that a pixel in an image is a specific green colour, it determines that it is part of the background, and deduces that the remainder of the image are people and objects in the foreground.

In this section, we will build a green screen program that can weave together the picture of an actor into a new background!

IMAGE PRIMER

Let's start by learning how images are represented in a computer. An image is simply a collection of **pixels**. As shown in Figure 4.4, each pixel forms a "dot" of colour of the image.

Each **pixel** is represented by a **colour**, which is stored as three **colour values** (Red, Green, Blue). You can think of the colour values as the amount of red, green, and blue light composing a particular colour. It is important to remember that each value ranges from 0 to 255.

So, for example, 0 for red and green and 255 for blue will produce the colour blue. You'll notice that since we use the convention of RGB, we can use a list of three integers to represent a colour without explicitly stating which value is for which colour. Figure 4.5 shows a few common colour RGB values.

> Note: Mixing colour values is not exactly like mixing paint. 255, 255, 255 does not equal black; it produces white. To help you remember, think about how white light contains the spectrum of colours.

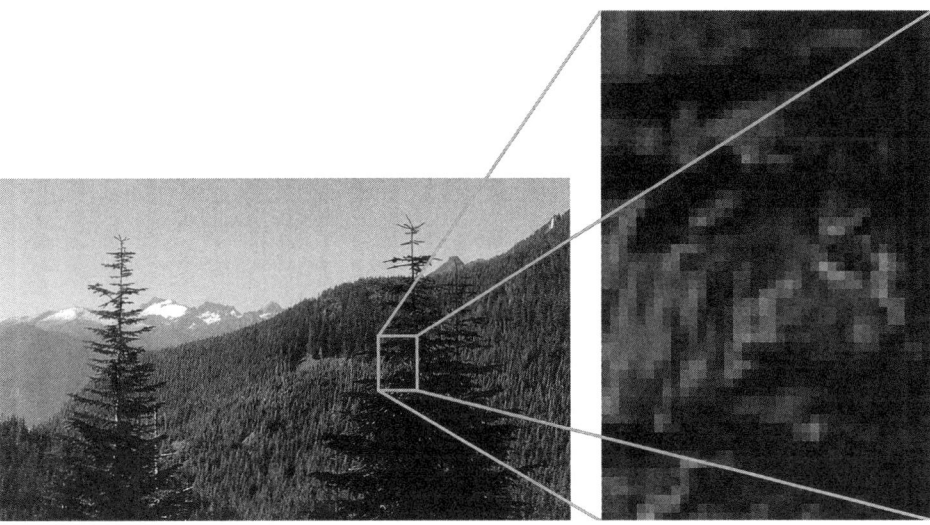

Figure 4.4 When you zoom in to a computer image, you'll see squares. Each square is a pixel.

Colour		Red	Green	Blue	
Red	■	255	0	0	◁ A red pixel [255, 0, 0]
Green	■	0	255	0	
Blue	■	0	0	255	
White	□	255	255	255	
Black	■	0	0	0	◁ A black pixel [0, 0, 0]
Yellow	□	255	255	0	

Figure 4.5 A few common colour values. Each colour value ranges from 0 to 255.

Besides knowing what colour pixels are in the image, a computer also needs to know *where* each pixel is in the image. Misplacing a pixel will result in a completely different image!

One way to store the pixels in their correct positions is to use a **two-dimensional matrix** where each entry of the matrix is a pixel and the position of the entry corresponds to the pixel's position in the image (Figure 4.6). We can use a 2D list (i.e., list of lists) to represent such a configuration, where each sublist stores a horizontal strip (row) of pixels, as shown in Figure 4.7.

ACCESSING PIXELS IN AN IMAGE

To start our exploration of images, download the supplied `kid-green.jpg` image and `csimage.py` file from our companion website. Then, place them in the same folder as the one in which you write your Python code.

Let's now explore the pixels in this image! In your own new Python program, start by importing the module `csimage`, similarly to how we imported the `random` module, to allow us to access a few helpful image processing functions. Use the function `csimage.getImage()` to load the image into your program as a **two-dimensional matrix**, described above.

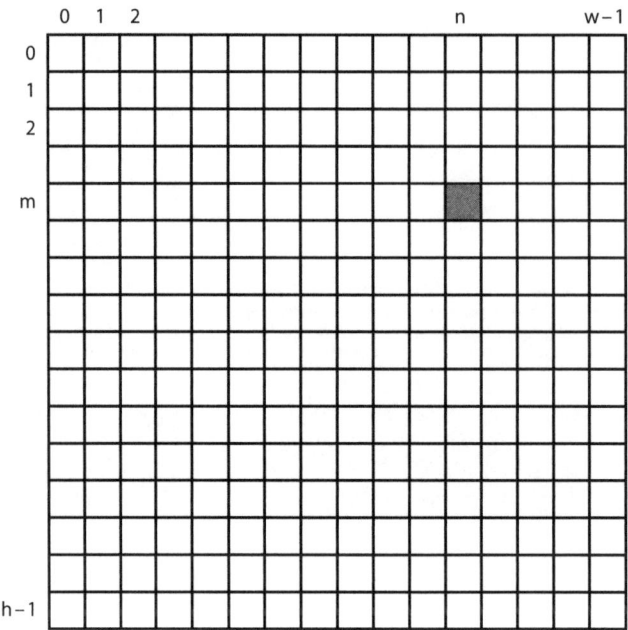

Figure 4.6 An image of width w and of height h. Note the counting starts with 0, as in lists.

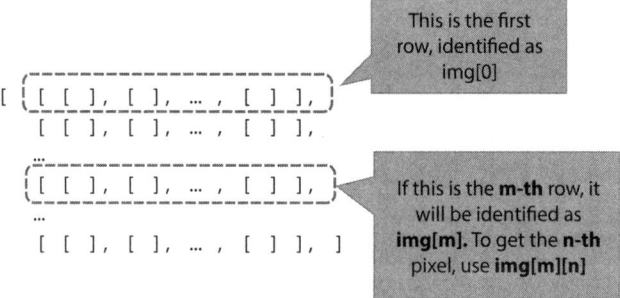

Figure 4.7 A 2D list (list of lists) called img is used to store the pixels of an image. If you have the first row entirely black and the second row entirely white, you'll have the list like this: [[[0,0,0], [0,0,0], ..., [0,0,0]], [[255,255,255], [255,255,255], ..., [255,255,255]], ...].

```
1   # Exploring Images
2   # Author:
3   # Date:
4
5   import csimage
6
7   # Open the image and store the contents into
8   # img as a 2D matrix
9   img = csimage.getImage("kid-green.jpg")
```

Next, let's access the top-left pixel at 0,0 and print out what its RGB values are. Given the picture in Figure 4.8, what RGB values do you expect?

```
1   # Exploring Images
2   # Author:
3   # Date:
4
5   import csimage
6
7   # Open the image and store the contents into
8   # img as a 2D matrix
9   img = csimage.getImage("kid-green.jpg")
10
11  # Get the pixel at location 0,0
12  pixel = img[0][0]
13
14  # Extract the colour values
15  # Each pixel is a list of 3 colour values
16  r = pixel[0]
17  g = pixel[1]
18  b = pixel[2]
19
20  print(r,g,b)
```

Figure 4.8 An image named kid-green.jpg with a kid on a solid colour (green) background (see companion website to view the original background colour in green).

The code below shows a shorter way to access the 0,0 pixel values directly. It is essentially equivalent to the code on the previous page.

```
1   # Exploring Images
2   # Author:
3   # Date:
4
5   import csimage
6
7   # Open the image and store the contents into
8   # img as a 2D matrix
9   img = csimage.getImage("kid-green.jpg")
10
11  # Get the pixel values at location 0,0
12  # and extract its RGB values
13  r = img[0][0][0]
14  g = img[0][0][1]
15  b = img[0][0][2]
16
17  print(r,g,b)
```

CHECKING THE COLOUR OF A PIXEL

Let's try to make our program decide whether the pixel is green. What happens when you run the code below?

```
1   # Exploring Images
2   # Author:
3   # Date:
4
5   import csimage
6
7   # Open the image and store the contents into
8   # img as a 2D matrix
9   img = csimage.getImage("kid-green.jpg")
10
11  # Get the pixel at location 0,0
12  # and extract its RGB values
13  pixel = img[0][0]
14  r = pixel[0]
15  g = pixel[1]
16  b = pixel[2]
17
18  # Test if this pixel is green
19  if r == 0 and g == 255 and b == 0:
20      print("The top-left pixel is green! It's background!")
21  else:
22      print("The top-left pixel is not green.")
```

You'll notice that even though we perceive the pixel as green, the RGB values may not be equal to 0, 255, 0 exactly. In fact, when you print the RGB values of the top-left pixel of the image, you'll see R = 15, G = 255, B = 21.

It turns out that a pixel can be green even if it has a little bit of blue and red, and slightly less than the maximum amount of green colour. So, to make your program less strict about what is meant by green, you can modify your conditional statement.

```
1    # Exploring Images
2    # Author:
3    # Date:
4
5    import csimage
6
7    # Open the image and store the contents into
8    # img as a 2D matrix
9    img = csimage.getImage("kid-green.jpg")
10
11   # Get the pixel at location 0,0
12   # and extract its RGB values
13   pixel = img[0][0]
14   r = pixel[0]
15   g = pixel[1]
16   b = pixel[2]
17
18   # Test if this pixel is green
19   if r < 100 and g > 200 and b < 100:
20       print("The top-left pixel is green! It's background!")
21   else:
22       print("The top-left pixel is not green.")
```

There you have it! You have a program that can check whether a pixel in your image is green or not! This will become handy later on.

FRUITFUL FUNCTIONS

We now have a program that can check a pixel to see whether it is green. But we want to check all the pixels in our image to decide whether they are part of the green screen. Imagine you have a big image with thousands or millions of pixels—you'll have to repeat this code thousands or millions of times!

How can we avoid copying/pasting code? We can begin by using a loop to save us the repetitions, and we can make it better by putting the checking steps into a repeatable unit. Recall our previous programs where we created functions, for example, to draw a cookie. In this program, we'd also like to write a function that takes a pixel to test and tells us whether it is green or not. The thing is, the functions we used previously can only "tell" us by printing a sentence to the display, which doesn't really help if we want to use this information for further processing of the image. We need another kind of function that can report the result, which can be used by the rest of the program.

In programming, there is a way to make a function return (i.e., report) a value. You have used this before; for example, random.choice(mylist) returned a random element from the list passed in as a parameter. When a function finishes its job, it returns a value that is either a simple value or a computed value stored in a variable. Since these functions not only compute something but also return something, we call them **fruitful functions**.

Here are some examples:

```
 1   # A fruitful function example
 2   # Author:
 3   # Date:
 4
 5   # A function that takes a numeric parameter
 6   # and returns whether it is greater than 1000
 7   # or not as a boolean
 8   def isGreaterThan1000(number):
 9     if number > 1000:
10       return True
11     else:
12       return False
13
14   testNumber = 999
15   if isGreaterThan1000(testNumber):
16     print(testNumber,"is greater than 1000.")
17   else:
18     print(testNumber,"is not greater than 1000.")
19
20   testNumber = 1050
21   if isGreaterThan1000(testNumber):
22     print(testNumber,"is greater than 1000.")
23   else:
24     print(testNumber,"is not greater than 1000.")
```

Since number > 1000 is actually a Boolean expression, a more compact way of writing the function above is as follows:

```
 1   # A fruitful function example
 2   # Author:
 3   # Date:
 4
 5   # A function that takes a numeric parameter
 6   # and returns whether it is greater than 1000
 7   # or not as a boolean
 8   def isGreaterThan1000(number):
 9     return number > 1000
```

In other words, the function will return True or False, representing whether or not the number passed in as a parameter is greater than 1,000. Here, True and False are Boolean values; in other words, they are a specific data type called Boolean, similar to int and string. Here is another example, this time returning a numeric value.

```
1   # Fruitful Function Example
2   # Author:
3   # Date:
4
5   # A function that takes as a numeric parameter
6   # and returns its value x100,
7   # only if the parameter > 0
8   def multiplier100(number):
9     if number > 0:
10      return number*100
11    print("Error: Sorry, please enter a positive number!")
12    return number
13
14  print(multiplier100(-4)) # Prints error then -4
15  print(multiplier100(4)) # Prints 400
```

As is the case with any other function, you can repeatedly call fruitful functions anywhere in the program after defining them. You can also use the returned value from a fruitful function as an input for another function.

The keyword `return` is a special keyword indicating that the function has completed its computation. Whenever the program sees this keyword it will stop the function and return the control back to whatever is calling this function, along with the value written next to `return` (if it exists). This means that you can have multiple return statements in a function as different exit points that could return different values.

So, the smarter way to test a large number of pixels for which ones are green is by implementing the check as a fruitful function. Note that the convention is to put function definitions at the top of the program, right after the import statements.

```
1   # Exploring Images
2   # Author:
3   # Date:
4
5   import csimage
6
7   def isGreen(pixel):
8       """
9       Returns True if the RGB values of pixel
10      combine to green, False otherwise
11      Input: a 3-valued list representing a pixel
12      and RGB values (ints)
13      Output: True if green, False otherwise
14      """
```

```
15      r = pixel[0]
16      g = pixel[1]
17      b = pixel[2]
18      return r < 100 and g > 200 and b < 100
19
20  # Test a few 3-valued lists to see
21  # how the isGreen function works
22  print(isGreen([255,255,255]))
23  print(isGreen([255,0,0]))
24  print(isGreen([0,255,0]))
```

SENSING GREEN

Now that we know how images are represented in computers and how we can sense the colour green in an image in a systematic way, let's put this knowledge in a program.

```
1   # Exploring Images
2   # Author:
3   # Date:
4
5   import csimage
6
7   def isGreen(pixel):
8       """
9       Returns True if the RGB values of pixel
10      combine to green, False otherwise
11      Input: a 3-valued list representing a pixel
12      and RGB values (ints)
13      Output: True if green, False otherwise
14      """
15      r = pixel[0]
16      g = pixel[1]
17      b = pixel[2]
18      return r < 100 and g > 200 and b < 100
19
20  # Open the image and store the contents
21  # into img as a 2D matrix
22  img = csimage.getImage("kid-green.jpg")
23
24  # Get the pixel at location 0,0
25  # and extract its RGB values
26  pixel = img[0][0]
27
28  # Test the top-left pixel of the image
29  # to see if it is green
30  if isGreen(pixel):
31      print("The top-left pixel is green! \
```

```
32        It's background!")
33   else:
34        print("The top-left pixel is not green.")
```

We are now ready to do some image magic with our green screen image!

4.2.3   Image Magic

In the previous section we covered some basics about image processing and how computers sense the colour green in an image. Now it's time to do some image magic using the green screen technique!

First, ensure you have downloaded the image in Figure 4.8 and copy the code below into the same directory on your computer:

> Don't worry if the code seems too complicated. We are just going to use the functions defined by the code. That's another advantage of functions: let others use them without worrying about the actual working mechanisms. Many programming languages support this kind of "offloading" of useful functions to another file and/or by another person.

```
1    # Name it as csimage.py
2    # Author:
3    # Date:
4    # Contains helper functions to wrap the Pygame
5    # image functions. Need an environment that has
6    # Pygame installed (e.g., Repl.it)
7
8    import pygame
9    import numpy
10
11   def getImage(filename):
12       """
13       Input: filename - string containing
14       image filename to open
15       Returns: 3d list of lists
16       (a height-by-width-by-3 list)
17       """
18       image = pygame.image.load(filename)
19       # do a transpose so its rows correspond to
20       # height of the image
21       return pygame.surfarray.array3d(image)\
22             .transpose(1, 0, 2).tolist()
23
24   def saveImage(pixels, filename):
25       """
```

```
26    Input: pixels - 3d list of lists of
27    RGB values (a height-by-width-by-3 list)
28            filename - string containing filename
29            to save image
30    Output: Saves a file containing pixels
31    """
32    # do a transpose so its rows correspond to
33    # width of the image (used by Pygame)
34    nparray = numpy.asarray(pixels)\
35            .transpose(1, 0, 2)
36    surf = pygame.surfarray.make_surface(nparray)
37    (width, height, colours) = nparray.shape
38    surf = pygame.display.set_mode((width, height))
39    pygame.surfarray.blit_array(surf, nparray)
40    pygame.image.save(surf, filename)
41
42 def showImage(pixels):
43    """
44    Input: pixels - 3d list of list of RGB values
45    (a height-by-width-by-3 list)
46    Output: show the image in a window
47    *this function uses the Pygame to display
48    a window in a not-so-conventional way
49    (without an event loop)
50    so it might appear frozen.
51    Suggested use: use it at the end of the program
52    to show how the image looks like
53    and make it stay by a this line:
54    print("Press enter to quit")
55    """
56    # do a transpose so its rows correspond to
57    # width of the image (used by Pygame)
58    nparray = numpy.asarray(pixels)\
59            .transpose(1, 0, 2)
60    surf = pygame.surfarray.make_surface(nparray)
61    (width, height, colours) = nparray.shape
62    pygame.display.init()
63    pygame.display.set_caption("CMPT120 - Image")
64    screen = pygame.display\
65            .set_mode((width, height))
66    screen.fill((225, 225, 225))
67    screen.blit(surf, (0, 0))
68    pygame.display.update()
```

Then copy this code into the same directory as the other two files:

```
1  # Replacing green with another colour
2  # Author:
3  # Date:
```

```
4
5   import csimage
6
7   def isGreen(pixel):
8       """
9       Returns True if the RGB values of pixel
10      combine to green, False otherwise
11      Assume "green" within 100 of 0,255,0
12      respectively
13      Input: a 3-valued list representing a pixel
14      and RGB values (ints)
15      Output: True if green, False otherwise
16      """
17      r = pixel[0]
18      g = pixel[1]
19      b = pixel[2]
20      return r < 100 and g > 200 and b < 100
21
22  # Open the green screen image
23  img = csimage.getImage("kid-green.jpg")
24
25  # Go through all the pixels
26  # in the green screen image
27  width = len(img[0]) # number of columns
28  height = len(img) # number of rows
29
30  for x in range(width):
31    for y in range(height):
32      # If a pixel is green, replace it with blue
33      # pixel colour at the same coordinates
34      pixel = img[y][x]
35      if isGreen(pixel):
36        img[y][x] = [0, 0, 255]
37
38  csimage.saveImage(img,"kid-blue.jpg")
```

Starting from line 25, this program goes through every pixel in the image using a nested for-loop, checks if a pixel is green, and replaces that pixel (stored in the img variable) with a blue pixel if so. Lastly, it saves the pixels into a new image file called kid-blue.jpg.

We use a nested for-loop to access every item in a multi-dimensional list because each "layer" of the for-loop guarantees all items in a dimension will be accessed once. So, for a 2D list we use a two-layer nested for-loop. If you are not sure how this works, add the statement print(str(x), str(y)) between lines 33 and 34 to see how x and y change to cover every item in the img variable.

Run this program and take a look at the result in the `kid-blue.jpg` file. As you will see, there is still a green outline of the kid in the image and a few green dots near her feet. The reason they are there is that while these pixels look green to us, they are not determined by the `isGreen` function as green. To address that we will have to adjust the values the function uses to compare the RGB colour values.

> As an exercise, experiment with the values the `isGreen` function uses to determine if a pixel is green or not, so that the green edges around the kid disappear. You can also change the replacement colour from blue to an other colour.

REPLACING BACKGROUND

Besides replacing the background (green pixels) with another colour, we can also replace it with another image, which is what the green screen technique really does.

Download the additional image below (`beach.jpg`) to the same directory as your other files.

Figure 4.9 A snowy beach.

Next, replace the code from the previous section with the following code:

```
1  # Exploring Images
2  # Author:
3  # Date:
```

```
4
5   import csimage
6
7   def isGreen(pixel):
8       """
9       Returns True if the RGB values of pixel
10      combine to green, False otherwise
11      Assume "green" within 100 of 0,255,0
12      respectively
13      Input: a 3-valued list representing a pixel
14      and RGB values (ints)
15      Output: True if green, False otherwise
16      """
17      r = pixel[0]
18      g = pixel[1]
19      b = pixel[2]
20      return r < 100 and g > 200 and b < 100
21
22  # Open the green screen image
23  img = csimage.getImage("kid-green.jpg")
24
25  # Open the beach image
26  beach = csimage.getImage("beach.jpg")
27
28  # Go through all the pixels
29  # in the green screen image
30  width = len(img[0]) # number of columns
31  height = len(img) # number of rows
32
33  for x in range(width):
34      for y in range(height):
35          # If a pixel is green, replace it with
36          # the beach image pixel colour
37          # at the same coordinates
38          pixel = img[y][x]
39          if isGreen(pixel):
40              img[y][x] = beach[y][x]
41
42  csimage.saveImage(img,"kid-beach.jpg")
```

For this code to work, the dimensions (width and height) of the beach image must be the same as that of the kid-green image.

Let's run this code and take a look at the result.

As you might have noticed, the only two differences between this code and the code in the previous section is that here 1) we read in the replacement image (beach.jpg) and 2) we replace each green pixel with the pixel from this image in the corresponding position

Figure 4.10 Replacing the green background with a beach!

(e.g., we use the top-left pixel of the beach image to replace the top-left green pixel of the kid image).

Congratulations! You have successfully performed the green screen technique using a computer program!

4.2.4   Cool Colours Module

Throughout our discussion about image processing and writing fruitful functions to do our image magic, we put all our function definitions in the same code file as the one in which we used them. What if we want to use these functions in other programs (e.g., write different programs to replace the green background with different things)?

One good way to do this is to put all the useful functions into a separate place where other programs can access them. In Python there is a way to do that: by creating **modules**. We have used modules before (remember random?). Now, let's learn to create one for ourselves!

PYTHON MODULES

A Python module is a file containing Python definitions and statements, including functions. Creating a module is a way for you to share your code with others. Typically you will name this file with a representative name so others will be able to figure out what this module does; for example, math.py would most likely contain functions that perform mathematical operations.

Let's organize the colour functions we have so far (along with a few more) into a Python module called coolcolours (thus the name coolcolours.py).

```python
1   # Name it as coolcolours.py
2   # Author:
3   # Date:
4   # Description: Contains functions for
5   # colour detection
6
7   """
8   Returns True if the RGB values of pixel
9   combine to red.
10  Assume "red" within 30 of 255,0,0 respectively
11  Input: a 3-valued list representing a pixel
12  and RGB values (ints)
13  Output: True if green, False otherwise
14  """
15  def isRed(pixel):
16    r = pixel[0]
17    g = pixel[1]
18    b = pixel[2]
19    return r > 225 and g < 30 and b < 30
20
21  """
22  Returns True if the RGB values of pixel
23  combine to green.
24  Assume "green" within 30 of 0,255,0 respectively
25  Input: a 3-valued list representing a pixel
26  and RGB values (ints)
27  Output: True if green, False otherwise
28  """
29  def isGreen(pixel):
30    r = pixel[0]
31    g = pixel[1]
32    b = pixel[2]
33    return r < 30 and g > 225 and b < 30
34
35  """
36  Returns True if the RGB values of pixel
37  combine to blue.
38  Assume "blue" within 30 of 0,0,255 respectively
39  Input: a 3-valued list representing a pixel
40  and RGB values (ints)
41  Output: True if green, False otherwise
42  """
43  def isBlue(pixel):
44    r = pixel[0]
45    g = pixel[1]
46    b = pixel[2]
47    return r < 30 and g < 30 and b > 225
48
```

```
49  """
50  Returns the colour of the pixel.
51  Using the assumptions for the RGB values
52  Input: a 3-valued list representing a pixel
53  and RGB values (ints)
54  Output: The string representing the colour
55  """
56  def getColour(pixel):
57    if isRed(pixel):
58      return "red"
59    elif isGreen(pixel):
60      return "green"
61    elif isBlue(pixel):
62      return "blue"
63    else:
64      return "other"
```

Now that we have put our colour functions into the `coolcolours` module, we can use them in any other program by including the module with the `import` keyword, followed by the module's name (the `.py` extension is not needed). Note that you have to import the module before you can use its functions. To avoid confusion (different modules might have some functions with the same name), call a function by first stating the module it belongs to and then its name, connected by a dot. So, to call the `isGreen` function from the `coolcolours` module, for example, you'll write this:

```
1  coolcolours.isGreen([255, 0, 0])
```

Here is our modified program replacing the background with another image using the `coolcolours` module (along with the `csimage` module for opening and saving image files). Pay attention to how the function `isGreen` is used in line 25:

```
1   # Exploring Images
2   # Author:
3   # Date:
4
5   import csimage
6   import coolcolours
7
8   # Open the green screen image
9   img = csimage.getImage("kid-green.jpg")
10
11  # Open the beach image
12  beach = csimage.getImage("beach.jpg")
13
14  # Go through all the pixels
15  # in the green screen image
16  width = len(img[0]) # number of columns
```

```
17  height = len(img) # number of rows
18
19  for x in range(width):
20    for y in range(height):
21      # If a pixel is green, replace it with
22      # the beach image pixel colour
23      # at the same coordinates
24      pixel = img[y][x]
25      if coolcolours.isGreen(pixel):
26        img[y][x] = beach[y][x]
27
28  csimage.saveImage(img,"kid-beach.jpg")
```

You can see that this code above is much shorter than the previous version, which is typically how we want our code to be: concise.

USING PYTHON MODULES

As demonstrated in the previous sections, the most typical way to use a Python module is to import it and call its functions using the *moduleName.functionName* convention.

However, Python allows you to use its modules in a few different ways to make the code easier to maintain. For example, if the module has a lot of functions and you only want to use a few of them, you can selectively import those you want:

```
1  from coolcolours import isGreen, isBlue
```

Here the from-import keyword combination imports the selected functions directly into your program but does not introduce the module itself. So **coolcolours** will not be recognized in your program and you can call only the imported functions, using their names directly:

```
1  # call the imported function directly
2  # without the module name
3  if isGreen([255, 0, 0]):
4      print("Green!")
5  else:
6      print("Not green.")
```

Importing selected functions is a slightly advanced way to use Python modules, so unless you know what you are doing it's best to import the whole module and call its functions via the *moduleName.functionName* convention. We include this information so that if you see other code importing selected functions, you'll know what they mean.

Another way to use Python modules is to make the module available to the program under a different name, which could be helpful if you want to name things in a certain way. For example, if instead of `coolcolours` you prefer `colourcheck`, you can assign this name to the `coolcolours` module when you are importing it:

```
1  import coolcolours as colourcheck
```

Then from this point on you can use its functions like this:

```
1  # call the imported function
2  # with a different module name
3  if colourcheck.isGreen([255, 0, 0]):
4      print("Green!")
5  else:
6      print("Not green.")
```

There you have it: a neat way to organize our code so not only can we use it for our-selves, but also pass it on to others to use, too! You should also be able to understand the meaning behind some advanced code that seemed to call functions from nowhere (e.g., `random.choice()`), and use existing Python modules on your own (e.g., `numpy`, a Python library that offers many useful mathematical tools).

4.2.5   Review Questions

Time to test how much you understand the content in this chapter. It's totally OK to go back and review!

THEORY AND UNDERSTANDING

- How is an image stored in a computer?
- In an image contained in a 2D list called `myImage`, how would you access the pixel located five pixels in and eight pixels down from the top left?
- How do you write a nested `for`-loop to print the RGB values for each pixel in an image contained in a 2D list called `yourImage`?
- What is a "fruitful function"? What separates it from other "non-fruitful functions"?
- What are the two modules/packages that are used in the `csimage` module?
- What is the name of a module relative to the name of the file containing it?
- What is the difference between a package and a module?

SYNTAX SELF-CHECK

What do the following functions and keywords mean:

- ```
  def multiplier_100(a):
      return (a*100)
  receive = multiplier_100(5)
  ```
- ```
  <init variable>
  while <boolean expression with variable>:
      <update variable>
  ```

- ```
def my_less_than(a,b):
    return a<b
if my_less_than(2,30):

    ....
```
- `my_3d_list[0][10][4]`
- `import cmpt120images`
- `import my_custom_module`

## 4.2.6    Practice Exercises

### CODING

Now it's time for you to practice by writing some code. When you are done, you can go to the Solutions section on our companion website to compare your answers with ours. Note that there can be many answers to the same question, so don't worry if yours are not the same as ours. The important things are that they produce the same results, and you are able to tell where the differences are and why both answers work.

### QUESTION 1

Write a function named `eliminateGreen(...)` that receives as an input parameter a list of RGB color values (where each RGB color is a three-value list) and returns a new list, where each element in the new list has the original RGB values but with no green component at all.

For example:
```
eliminateGreen([[100,100,100], [10,255,0], [100,35,255],
[10,0,200]])
```
should return the new list:
```
[[100,0,100], [10,0,0], [100,0,255], [10,0,200]]
```

## 4.3    DRAWING TREES

In the computer-generated image in Figure 4.11, what are some elements that may be well suited to be generated by a computer, rather than be drawn by hand?

While the field of computer graphics deals with the artistic rendering of many complex aspects, including lighting, reflection, and texture, in this chapter we'll look at something simpler and see how we can draw beautiful, complex trees with just a little bit of code, using a programming technique called recursion.

## 4.3.1    Learning Outcomes

At the end of this unit, you will be able to ...

### RECURSION

- know the basic elements of a recursive function
- analyze a recursively drawn tree in `turtle`
- write a simple recursive function (e.g., to draw concentric circles) that does not return any value
```

Figure 4.11 A computer-generated scene with a tree.

- understand the difference between executing a line of code before a recursive call and after a recursive call
- apply the three laws of recursion to write or analyze a basic fruitful function
- write a number of recursive functions (e.g., to calculate factorial, produce sum of a list, reverse a string, check if a string is a palindrome)

4.3.2   Intro to Recursion

What is recursion? In Figure 4.12 you'll find a few examples of recursion in the real world. Whether it's romanesco broccoli, the 1904 Droste cocoa tin, or Matryoshka dolls, we can see examples of recursion in real life: a vegetable, image or object that contains some version of itself.

In computer science, we call a function recursive if it contains a call to the function itself. You will see an example shortly. Recursion is a concept that is not strictly necessary to know in order to solve problems using code—we often use recursion to perform repetition, and in many cases, loops can do the same job. However, it's an alternative way that may result in more elegant or cleaner code, and being able to think about recursive algorithms can open up new approaches and ideas.

REVISITING THE COUNTDOWN EXAMPLE

Consider an example problem we looked at earlier in this book. How would you create a program that would count down from 10 to 1? More specifically, can you write a function countdown that would accept an argument n, and print a countdown until 1?

```
1  # Countdown Print
2  # Author:
3  # Date:
4  # Use a loop to print numbers counting down
5
6  def countdown(n):
7     for i in range(n,0,-1):
```

```
 8      print(i)
 9
10   countdown(10)
```

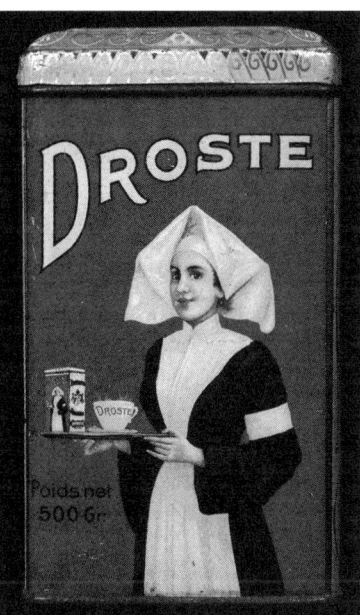

Figure 4.12 Left: An image of a romanesco broccoli, by Ivar Leidus, CC BY-SA 4.0, https://creativecommons.org/licenses/by-sa/4.0, via Wikimedia Commons. Right: An image of a box cover design containing an image of the same box, by Alf van Beem, CC0, via Wikimedia Commons.

In the code above, we use a loop to print from n all the way down to (but not including) 0, decrementing by 1 each time. Now, it is also possible to write a function that achieves the same result using recursion.

In the code below, the function countdown_rec prints n (line 10), and then calls itself using the parameter of n-1 (line 11). Notice that if n is ever 1, it prints n and no longer calls itself (line 8).

```
 1   # Recursive Print
 2   # Author:
 3   # Date:
 4   # Use recursion to print numbers counting down
 5
 6   def countdown_rec(n):
 7     if n == 1: # Base case
 8       print(n)
 9     else:
10       print(n)
11       countdown_rec(n-1)
12
13   countdown_rec(10)
```

This code contains the three pieces necessary for a recursive function:

- It calls itself (line 11); this is known as the "recursive call"
- It has a base case (line 7); this helps the function know when to stop recursing
- In the call to itself (line 11, parameter), it moves towards the base case

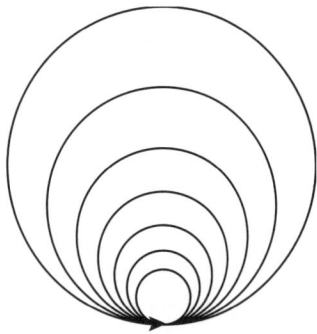

So far, this code doesn't necessary seem simpler or cleaner than the loop code, but we'll see some examples later where you will notice the difference!

A SIMILAR EXAMPLE USING TURTLE TO DRAW A VORTEX!

Here is another example, but in this case using turtle to draw the vortex image below. Run the code to see how the code is executed. You will see that the circles are drawn one by one, starting from the outside.

Without recursion, we can draw the vortex using a loop, updating the size of the circles progressively to 75% of the previous size:

Figure 4.13 Using recursion to draw a vortex.

```
1   # Vortex with Loop
2   # Author:
3   # Date:
4   # Draw a vortex using circles and recursion
5
6   import turtle
7   pete = turtle.Turtle()
8
9   def vortex(initialSize):
10    currentSize = initialSize
11    for i in range(7,0,-1):
12      pete.circle(currentSize)
13      currentSize = currentSize*.75
14
15  vortex(120)
```

Now, see below for a **recursive function** that creates an equivalent turtle image. It contains a base case (line 12) and a call to itself (line 16). Notice that only the else condition in lines 14–16 is executed until the last and smallest circle is drawn. After that, the base case (line 12), which does nothing (using the keyword pass), is triggered; In the base case, vortex is not called, and the drawing stops. The structure is very similar to the countdown code above.

```
1   # Recursive Vortex
2   # Author:
3   # Date
4   # Draw a vortex using circles and recursion,
5   # from largest to smallest
6
7   import turtle
```

```
 8  pete = turtle.Turtle()
 9
10  def vortex(size):
11    # Base case
12    if size <= 20:
13      pass # Do nothing
14    else:
15      pete.circle(size)
16      vortex(size*0.75)
17
18  vortex(120)
```

DIGGING DEEPER . . .

Now that we've seen some basic examples of recursive functions, we should try and understand how recursion works under the hood. Run the following code and see what it prints. Are you surprised by the output? What is different about this code from the previous `countdown` function?

```
 1  # Countdown Revisited
 2  # Author:
 3  # Date
 4  # Use recursion to print numbers counting down
 5
 6  def countdown_revisited(n):
 7    if n == 1: # Base case
 8      print(n)
 9    else:
10      countdown_revisited(n-1)
11      print(n)
12
13  countdown_revisited(10)
```

In this case, you will notice that the code prints out 1 to 10 (1, 2, 3, …, 9, 10) on separate lines instead of a countdown (10, 9, 8, …, 2, 1). The main difference between `countdown_revisited` above and the first `countdown_rec` above is that lines 10 and 11 are swapped. What's happening?

Essentially, each call to `countdown_revisited` puts the currently executing function on hold. For instance, when `countdown_revisited(10)` is executing and reaches line 10, it calls `countdown_revisited(9)` (because n=10 and n-1=9). At that point, `countdown_revisited(10)` is put on hold while `countdown_revisited(9)` proceeds. In other words, `countdown_revisited(10)` waits until `countdown_revisited(9)` finishes. Only when the function in line 10 finishes can it proceed to the next line of code in line 11.

Now, consider that we progressively put these functions on hold until we reach the base case. For instance, we follow the same logic above and continue to `countdown_revisited(2)`, which is put on hold while it waits for `countdown_revisited(1)`to finish. When `countdown_revisited(1)` is called, it ends up in the base case (line 7) since, finally, n is equal to 1. At that point, thanks to line 8, the value of n is printed to the screen (i.e., the number 1) and the function `countdown_revisited(1)` terminates.

This `countdown_revisited(1)` is called by line 10 of `countdown_revisited` `(2)`, so when `countdown_revisited(1)` terminates, the next line of code is run (line 11), which prints 2. After printing (line 11), `countdown_revisited(2)` terminates and gives back control to `countdown_revisited(3)`, which was waiting for line 10 to finish. This process continues until `countdown_revisited(9)` terminates and proceeds to print 10.

In this way, you can see that 1, 2, 3, ..., 9, 10 are printed to the screen. The same idea applies to this piece of code, which swaps line 15 and line 16. When you run the following code, you will see that the picture is drawn from the smallest inner circle progressively to the largest outer circle. Each call from `vortex(120)`, to line 15's `vortex(90)` → `vortex(67.5)`→ ... is put on hold until the base case. Once the base case is reached, the turtle begins to draw using line 16, then terminates progressively from smallest size to largest.

```
1   # Vortex Revisited
2   # Author:
3   # Date:
4   # Draw a vortex using circles and recursion,
5   # from smallest to largest
6
7   import turtle
8   pete = turtle.Turtle()
9
10  def vortex(size):
11      # Base case
12      if size <= 20:
13          pass # Do nothing
14      else:
15          vortex(size*0.75)
16          pete.circle(size)
17  vortex(120)
```

4.3.3   Recursion Revisited

We began this chapter by looking at trees and considering that it could be nice to have a computer draw their complex, repetitive structure. We found that recursion can be found in nature, where an object contains smaller versions of itself (e.g., an onion, romanesco broccoli, etc.) Trees also tend to follow this structure, where a tree or branch contains smaller versions of itselves.

We're now ready to use recursion to construct a program that can draw a beautiful tree! We will start by drawing a basic tree (left) and then add a few more bells and whistles to achieve a fancy tree (right).

The Basic Recursive Tree code below draws a branch (line 14), then turns left (line 17) to draw a smaller subtree. Once that smaller subtree (line 18) is finished drawing, it

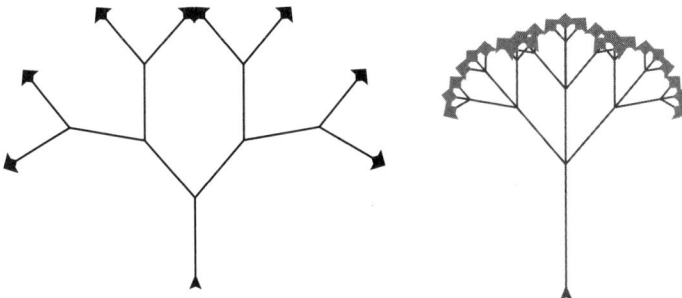

Figure 4.14 Left: A basic recursive tree. Right: A fancy recursive tree.

turns right and draws another smaller subtree (line 22). The function parameter `level` is used as a control parameter to know when we should stop recursing, i.e., when level is 0. We can see that this code contains the *three* basic ingredients for a recursive program:

- At least one recursive call to itself (line 18, and also line 21)
- A base case (line 9)
- The recursive calls move the state toward the base case (here, we refer to the argument n-1 in lines 18 and 21, moving towards n==0)

```
1   # Basic Recursive Tree
2   # Author:
3   # Date:
4   # Draw a basic tree using recursion
5
6   import turtle
7
8   def draw_tree(level):
9     # Base case - leaf
10    if level == 0:
11      bob.stamp()
12    else:
13      # Draw a branch
14      bob.forward(60)
15
16      # Turn slightly left and draw a mini tree
17      bob.left(40)
18      draw_tree(level-1)
19      # Turn to the right and draw a mini tree
20      bob.right(80)
21      draw_tree(level-1)
22
23      # Turn back to the center and move back
24      bob.left(40)
25      bob.back(60)
```

```
26
27  bob = turtle.Turtle()
28  bob.left(90)
29  draw_tree(4)
```

Run the Basic Recursive Tree code and watch the turtle to see how the program executes. It is helpful to watch the drawing happening in real time, as you'll see that all of the left subtrees are drawn before commencing any right branches.

FANCY RECURSIVE TREE

Now that we've seen how to draw a basic tree, we can add a few more details. For example, what if we want the branches to gradually get shorter as we move towards the leaves?

In the Fancy Recursive Tree example below, we have added an additional parameter to our function, to change an aspect of our drawing. The second parameter called branch_length is divided by 1.61 (a number close to the "golden ratio") each time the function calls itself (e.g., line 20). Instead of hard-coding the branch length as 60, as in our previous example in line 14, we send the second value as a fraction of itself. Note that we don't need to worry about this parameter moving closer to the base case! Our base case is dependent only on the level parameter.

Other additional changes to this program are as follows:

- Each branch splits into three branches (lines 20, 23 and 26) instead of two. The turning angles have also been adjusted to produce the effect of creating a subtree on the left, the middle and then the right.
- We have changed the colour of the trunk/branches (lines 13 and 36) and leaves (line 11).
- We have increased the drawing speed (line 34) and changed the thickness of the pen (line 35)

```
1   # Fancy Recursive Tree
2   # Author:
3   # Date:
4   # Draw a fancy tree using recursion
5
6   import turtle
7
8   def draw_tree(level,branch_length):
9     # Base case - leaf
10    if level == 0:
11      bob.color("purple")
12      bob.stamp()
13      bob.color("brown")
14    else:
15      # Draw a branch
16      bob.forward(branch_length)
17
18      # Turn slightly left and draw a mini tree
19      bob.left(40)
```

```
20      draw_tree(level-1,branch_length/1.61)
21      # Turn to the middle and draw a mini tree
22      bob.right(40)
23      draw_tree(level-1,branch_length/1.61)
24      # Turn back to the right and draw a mini tree
25      bob.right(40)
26      draw_tree(level-1,branch_length/1.61)
27
28      # Go back
29      bob.left(40)
30      bob.back(branch_length)
31
32  bob = turtle.Turtle()
33  bob.left(90)
34  bob.speed(500)
35  bob.width(2)
36  bob.color("brown")
37  draw_tree(5,120)
```

In this section we use recursion to draw images, and the functions do not return any values. Recursion can also be combined with fruitful functions (i.e., functions with a return statement) to produce some interesting effects. Let's look at a common example inspired by mathematics.

FRUITFUL RECURSION

Factorial of n (also written as n!) is defined as the product of all positive integers less than or equal to n. For instance, 4! = 4x3x2x1 = 24. 0! is defined as 1.

We can use recursion to define the `factorial` function, as below. In our base case of 0 (lines 7–8), the function returns `1`, which follows our definition of factorial. However, how do we define the recursive case?

We notice a useful substructure in our example above. Since 3! is defined as 3x2x1, we can see that 4! = 4x3!.

Using this substructure, we can write our recursive call as in line 11 of the code below. In our recursive tree example we could assume that a call to `draw_tree(n-1)`draws a slightly smaller tree, and here we can assume that `factorial(n-1)` returns factorial of n-1.

At the end, when we call `factorial(4)`, line 11 is run and waits for `factorial(3)` to complete, which waits for `factorial(2)` to complete, and so on. All of these functions return the value we expect and produce the desired product.

```
1  # Recursive Factorial
2  # Author:
3  # Date:
4  # Recursively calculate the factorial of n
5
6  def factorial(n):
7      # Base case
8      if n == 0:
```

```
 9        return 1
10    else:
11        return n*factorial(n-1)
12
13  print(factorial(4))
```

4.3.4   Review Questions

Time to test how much you understand the content in this chapter. It's totally OK to go back and review!

THEORY AND UNDERSTANDING

- What are some non-computing examples of recursion?
- What does recursion allow us to do?
- Give three components of a recursive function.
- When a recursive function calls itself, what must we make sure of?
- What happens if a recursive function doesn't have a base case?
- Consider the functions defined below. What does doer(3) print? What does waiter(3) print?

```
1  def doer(n):
2    if n == 0:
3        pass
4    else:
5        print(n)
6        doer(n-1)
```

```
1  def waiter(n):
2    if n == 0:
3        pass
4    else:
5        waiter(n-1)
6        print(n)
```

- Do all parameters in a recursive function need to be used for controlling the end of recursion?
- What is a classic math problem that can be solved with fruitful recursion?

4.3.5   Practice Exercises

CODING

Now it's time for you to practice by writing some code. When you are done, you can go to the Solutions section on our companion website to compare your answers with ours. Note that there can be many answers to the same question, so don't worry if yours are not the same as ours. The important things are that they produce the same results, and you are able to tell where the differences are and why both answers work.

SUMMING NUMBERS

Define and test a recursive function `sum_recursive(n)` that takes a positive integer as a parameter and returns n + (n-1) + (n-2) + ... + 2 + 1. Can you also write a non-recursive version of this function?

TRIANGLE VORTEX

Draw a triangle vortex similar to the one below using recursion. Hint: First define a function `triangle(n)` that takes a parameter *n* defining the length of a side. You may need to ensure that your turtle is facing the same direction at the end of the function as at the beginning of the function. You can then use this `triangle` function within your recursive `triangle_vortex` function.

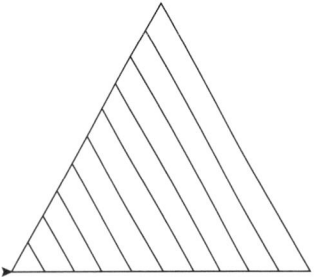

Figure 4.15 A triangle vortex.

EXTRA FANCY RECURSIVE TREE

Challenge yourself! Can you create a version of the Fancy Recursive Tree that randomly selects the angles of the branches? You may use the `random.randint(a,b)` function, which returns a random number between a and b, inclusive. Hint: You may need to store some values. You can also try to randomly change the length of each branch.

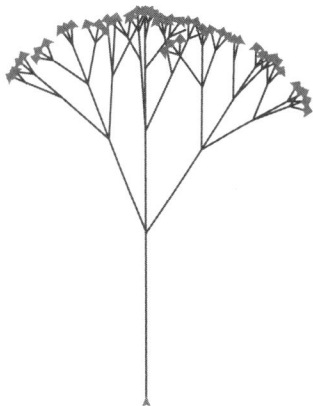

Figure 4.16 An extra fancy recursive tree using random values.

Internet and Big Data

Computers are very good at handling data quickly and accurately, as long as you give them clear instructions. In this chapter you'll learn some of the fundamental algorithms to process large amounts of data. The programs you'll be writing include:

- Linear Search (for shoes)
- Higher-Lower Number Guessing Game
- Binary Search
- Swapping hats
- Selection sort (with timer)
- Many locations
- Palindrome Checker

We will begin with a motivating example of searching through a large number of shoes in a store, and see how our intuition can produce a computational search algorithm. In particular, we'll see how sorting data (or shoes) can unlock new and improved search algorithms. In addition to searching and sorting algorithms, we'll introduce the concepts of map, filter, and reduce, which are used in modern applications on the web.

CS topics in this unit:

- List indexing and slicing
- Linear search
- Binary search
- Selection sort
- Swapping values
- Merge sort
- Higher order functions
- Map, filter, and reduce

5.1 SEARCHING

Searching is a common activity you may perform every day using search engines on the web. Behind the scenes, there are powerful algorithms that allow us to search for keywords in web pages, or information in databases. Let's explore this concept of search. We'll learn two search algorithms: linear search and binary search.

5.1.1   Learning Outcomes

At the end of this unit, you will be able to …

SEARCHING

- write a linear search function with various return types (e.g., Boolean, index of unique found element, indices of all found elements)
- recognize a binary search and write the code for it
- write the code for a recursive binary search

5.1.2   Linear Search

Imagine you've entered a shoe shop and are looking for a pair in size 9. This shop is new so the shoes are not yet organized by their sizes. How could you search for what you need? Let's consider a simple Python analogy for searching, which would be looking for a given value in a list.

Challenge: Given a list of integers (e.g., of shoe sizes), and a search term (e.g., 9), can you write a function that will return the Boolean value `True` if the search term is in the list, and `False` otherwise?

Figure 5.1 What is the algorithm for finding a shoe in your size when the shoes are disorganized? What would be your algorithm if the shoes were sorted?

```
1   # Linear Search - Boolean
2   # Author:
3   # Date:
```

```
 4
 5  # Input: a list of integers or strings
 6  # Output: True if search_term is in list
 7  #          False otherwise
 8  def search(input_list,search_term):
 9    for item in input_list:
10      if item == search_term:
11        return True
12    return False
13
14  # Test your search function with a
15  # simple list and a search term of 5
16  print(search([1,2,3,4,5],5))
```

In the example above, we used a for-loop to iterate through our list and return True as soon as the search term was found. Note how we have a default return value, False, if the list were searched entirely and True were not returned (remember, return ends the execution of the function).

Now, can you create a function with the same input and output requirements, but using a while-loop?

```
 1  # Linear Search - Boolean (while)
 2  # Author:
 3  # Date:
 4
 5  # Input: a list of integers or strings
 6  # Output: True if search_term is in list
 7  #          False otherwise
 8  def search_while(input_list, search_term):
 9    i = 0
10    input_list_length = len(input_list)
11    while i < input_list_length:
12      if input_list[i] == search_term:
13        return True
14      i+=1
15    return False
16
17  # Test your search function with a
18  # simple list and a search term of 5
19  print(search([1,2,3,4,5],5))
```

Next, imagine that you want to know more than whether or not your shoe is in stock (True/False). Rather, you want the actual location of the shoe. In our Python example, we could define the problem as follows.

Challenge: Given a list of numbers (e.g., of shoe sizes) and a search term, can you write a function that will return the **index** of the search term, and None otherwise? Try it!

```
1   # Linear Search - Index
2   # Author:
3   # Date:
4
5   # Input: a list of integers or strings
6   # Output: first index where search_term is found
7   #         None, if not in the list
8   def search_index(input_list,search_term):
9     i = 0
10    while i < len(input_list):
11      if input_list[i] == search_term:
12        return i
13      i += 1
14    return None
15
16  # Test your search function with
17  # some simple lists and search terms
18  print(search([1,2,3,4,5],5))
19  print(search(["a","b","c","d"],"c")
20  print(search(["a","b","c","d"],"x")
21  print(search([],"x") # Test the empty list
```

All three methods above, using simple looping through a list to find a search item, are variants of **Linear Search**.

5.1.3   Binary Search

In the last section, we learned how to do the simplest search, called Linear Search. This search is flexible because we can run it on any data; there is no assumption on how the data is organized. Unfortunately, this also means your search could be very slow if your search item happens to be the last item you look at or if it does not exist.

How do we handle this problem in real life? When you walk into a shoe shop, are shoes organized, and how? Whether it's a shoe shop or a library, items are usually **sorted**.

Figure 5.2 We can use a binary search to find a shoe, only if they are sorted.

Although it will take some time to do the initial tidying up, or **sorting** (which we'll look at in Section 5.2), a sorted list will make looking up an item much quicker later, every single time.

BINARY SEARCH

Let's assume our data is sorted, from lowest to highest. This data organization allows us to use a search algorithm called **Binary Search**. Here's the intuition. Have you every played the High-Low game? In this game, your friend should choose a number between 1 and 100. Your job is to guess their number, and they will tell you if you need to go higher or lower, and so on. What is the optimal strategy for choosing the number? Would you choose 99, then 98, and so on? One common strategy is choose the middle number of the set of numbers you haven't explored yet. So, for example, the game might go like this:

- I guess 50. (Higher!)
- I guess 75. (Lower!)
- I guess 63. (Higher!)
- I guess 69. (Higher!)
- I guess 72. (You're right!)

The same intuition helps us write the algorithm for **Binary Search**, as explained below. We use two variables to help us keep track of the part of our list we haven't explored yet. Then, we continue checking the middle of that list until we find our number. As in our previous section on Linear Search, we can check for presence of the item (i.e., return `True` or `False`) or return the index (i.e., location) of the term in the list.

Remember, the data needs to be sorted from lowest to highest for this code to work.

```
1   # Binary Search
2   # Author:
3   # Date:
4
5   # Returns True if in the list, false otherwise
6   def binarySearch(input_list,search_term):
7     # Keep track of active search space
8     low = 0
9     high = len(input_list)-1 # last element index
10
11    while low <= high:
12      # Check the midpoint of active search space
13      midpoint = (low+high)//2 # round down to the nearest int
14      # If it's the search term, return True
15      if input_list[midpoint] == search_term:
16        return True
17
18      else:
19        # Otherwise, modify search space based on if
20        # midpoint is lower/higher than search_term
21        if search_term < input_list[midpoint]:
22          high = midpoint - 1
23        else:
```

```
24              low = midpoint + 1
25      return False
26
27  testlist = [0, 1, 2, 8, 13, 17, 19, 32, 42, 80]
28
29  print(binarySearch(testlist,13))
30  print(binarySearch(testlist,3))
```

Challenge: How would you modify the code above to work for a list that is sorted from highest to lowest?

Challenge: Both Linear Search and Binary Search work on a sorted list. Given the same sorted list, calculate the number of items we need to check in the Linear Search vs. Binary Search versions. How much better is Binary Search compared to Linear Search? In which cases? While out of the scope of this book, formal definitions and analyses exist to answer this question.

5.1.4   Review Questions

Time to test how much you understand the content in this chapter. It's totally OK to go back and review!

THEORY AND UNDERSTANDING

- What were the names of the searching algorithms we learned in this section?
- In your own words, describe how each of these algorithms works for searching.
- If a list is sorted, what kind of search can we do?
- What indices do we need to keep track of for binary search?

5.1.5   Practice Exercises

CODING

Now it's time for you to practice by writing some code. When you are done, you can go to the Solutions section on our companion website to compare your answers with ours. Note that there can be many answers to the same question, so don't worry if yours are not the same as ours. The important things are that they produce the same results, and you are able to tell where the differences are and why both answers work.

MANY LOCATIONS

Given a list of integers and a search term, write a search function that will return a list containing **all indices** where the search term can be found. For example, if the list is [3,2,6,3,4], and your search term is 3, the function should return [0,3]. If the search term cannot be found, return an empty list [ ]. Your solution should use the append function (the append function inserts one item to the end of an existing list. For example, if we call mylist.append(4)on mylist, which is [1,2,3], mylist becomes [1,2,3,4]). You must write at least three test cases, and cannot make any assumptions about the ordering of the data.

```
1   def search_multiple(integer_list,search_term):
```

PALINDROME CHECKER

You are building an app that can suggest interesting names for companies. Write a function `is_palindrome(`*word*`)` that uses a loop to check whether *word* is a palindrome, i.e., spelled the same forwards and backwards. It should return `True` if the word is a palindrome and `False` if it is not.

Challenge: Write this function using recursion.

5.2   SORTING

Another common activity you may perform when it comes to a large amount of data is to sort the data, that is, organize the data in a particular order (e.g., from smallest to largest). Sorted data is useful because we can easily find out interesting information about the data, for example, what is the smallest value? what is the largest value? and what is the median value? We'll learn two sort algorithms: Selection Sort and Merge Sort.

5.2.1   Learning Outcomes

At the end of this unit, you will be able to …

SORTING

- swap different elements in a list
- use `range()` with multiple parameters to iterate over a sublist, or to iterate backwards over a list
- identify and write the code for Selection Sort
- describe the general approach and functioning of Merge Sort

5.2.2   Selection Sort

In the previous section, we wanted to search for our pair of shoes and found out that if our data were sorted, we could find our item more quickly on average. But, how can we write an algorithm to sort our data in the first place? Let's consider the real-life problem of sorting playing cards.

Consider the image `below`. How would you go about sorting your hand of cards, given how the cards are arranged? One possible way is to select the smallest number cards (in this case, the 2s) and move them to the front. Then select the next smallest number cards (the 3s) and move them in between your 2s and the rest of the hand. Then, select the next smallest number (the 4s) and move them between your 3s and the rest of the hand. After doing this a few times, you will start to notice that you are maintaining a sorted part of your hand (on the left), and the unsorted portion (on the right).

This is the underlying algorithm for the **Selection Sort**. The only difference is that, with our list, we will make space for the smallest card by swapping it with the first card in the unsorted portion. (Insertion is also a tool available to us, but let's consider swapping as a simple constraint for now.)

SWAPPING NEEDS A TEMPORARY VARIABLE

In order for us to implement our Selection Sort, we first need to learn a paradigm for swapping elements in a list, which will be our key tool for sorting our list. This is

Figure 5.3 A common example used for sorting is a hand of playing cards.

not straightforward. Imagine trying to swap hats with another person in a step-by-step manner:

1. First, your friend would need to take off their hat, perhaps placing it on a table.
2. Then, you'd place your hat on their head.
3. Now that your head is bare, your friend can pick up their hat from the table and put it on your head.

Figure 5.4 Imagine trying to swap hats: What is the algorithm?

The main takeaway is that you need an extra spot to store your friend's hat (e.g., the table) during all of this hat-swapping business! In code, we can call this extra storage space "temp", since we only need the space temporarily during the swap.

```
1   # Swapping items in a list
2   # Author:
3   # Date:
4
5   # Create a list
6   numbers = [0,1,2,3,4]
7   print(numbers)
8
9   # Swap the numbers at index 0 and 1
10  tempNum = numbers[1]     # Make item 1 copy
11  numbers[1] = numbers[0] # item 1 <- item 0
12  numbers[0] = tempNum     # item 0 <- item 1 copy
13  print(numbers)
14
15  # Python has an easy swap trick
16  numbers[0],numbers[1] = numbers[1],numbers[0]
17  print(numbers)
```

Now, while it's important to understand how swapping works under the hood, in Python there is a straightforward syntax to swap elements in a list (line 16). We will use this syntax for all examples going forward.

SELECTION SORT

Now that we have learned how to swap, let's examine how to implement this in code. First, note the main steps:

1. Search for the minimum value in our unsorted portion of the list (lines 11–19). This requires first setting a default minimum (i.e., the first element in the sorted portion) (line 12) and then seeing if there is anything smaller in the rest of the unsorted list. If there is, then we update our minimum value and its location (lines 18–19)
2. Swap the minimum item we found with the first element of the unsorted list (lines 22–23)

Repeat the above two steps over all the elements in the list.

```
1   # Selection Sort
2   # Author:
3   # Date:
4
5   # Input: unsorted list of integers
6   # Output: sorted list of integers
7   def selectionSort(num_list):
8     # Loop len(num_list) times
9     for i in range(len(num_list)):
10
11      # Set first unsorted element as minimum
12      min_num = num_list[i]
13      min_index = i
```

```
14
15      # See if there is a smaller element
16      for j in range(i+1,len(num_list)):
17        if num_list[j] < min_num:
18          min_num = num_list[j]
19          min_index = j
20
21      # Swap min with first element in sublist
22      num_list[min_index],num_list[i] = \
23          num_list[i],num_list[min_index]
24
25  test_input = [39,2,103,42,50,61]
26
27  selectionSort(test_input)
28  print(test_input)
```

For fun, we will also use the time module to calculate how long our sort takes to run. This requires three elements:

1. Importing the time module (line 4)
2. Using time.time() to get the current time before (line 28) and after (line 31) our sort procedure
3. Calculating the elapsed time (line 34)

```
1   # Timing our sort
2   # Author:
3   # Date:
4   import time
5
6   # Input: unsorted list of integers
7   # Output: sorted list of integers
8   def selectionSort(num_list):
9     # Loop len(num_list) times
10    for i in range(len(num_list)):
11
12      # Set first unsorted element as minimum
13      min_num = num_list[i]
14      min_index = i
15
16      # See if there is a smaller element
17      for j in range(i+1,len(num_list)):
18        if num_list[j] < min_num:
19          min_num = num_list[j]
20          min_index = j
21
22      # Swap min with first element in sublist
23      num_list[min_index],num_list[i] = \
```

```
24              num_list[i],num_list[min_index]
25
26  test_input = [39,2,103,42,50,61]
27
28  t1 = time.time()
29  print(t1)
30  selectionSort(test_input)
31  t2 = time.time()
32  print(t2)
33  print(test_input)
34  print("Our sort took",t2-t1,"seconds to run.")
```

ASIDE: SLICING OR INDEXING?

Let's take a closer look at how we decided to implement finding the minimum value in the sublists (unsorted portion of the list) above. You might think that slicing using the : operator would be a good way to create sublists (line 5, below, Method 1). But this procedure creates a new copy of the sublist in memory each time you try to find the minimum value! If your list contained a million elements, this could create a million copies of the list, which is very space/memory inefficient.

Because of this, we suggest using indexing (line 10, below, Method 2) to access the sublist and uncover its minimum value.

```
1   # How can we iterate over a sublist of numbers?
2   numbers = [0,1,2,3,4]
3
4   # Method 1 (slicing) creates a sublist copy
5   sublist = numbers[2:]
6   for num in sublist:
7     print(num)
8
9   # Method 2 (indexing) does not create a copy
10  for i in range(2,len(numbers)):
11    print(numbers[i])
```

Now you know how to sort your data and can take full advantage of the Binary Search algorithm! There are more searching and sorting algorithms out there, which are even more clever and efficient. Let's explore an even faster sorting algorithm, called **Merge Sort**.

5.2.3 Merge Sort

Merge Sort is much faster way to sort lists compared to Selection Sort, especially when the number of items to sort is large.

Let's start with an example to get the intuition behind the Merge Sort algorithm. Suppose you were given two lists of numbers, and each list was already sorted from smallest to largest.

| 8 | 13 | 16 | 22 | 74 | 94 | 99 |

| −3 | −1 | 36 | 73 | 80 | 86 |

Figure 5.5 Two sorted piles of cards, here depicted as two sequences of increasing numbers.

How would you combine the two lists into one sorted list?

MERGE ALGORITHM

One possibility is to start from the beginning of each list. Then, you would pick the smaller item and add it to a result list.

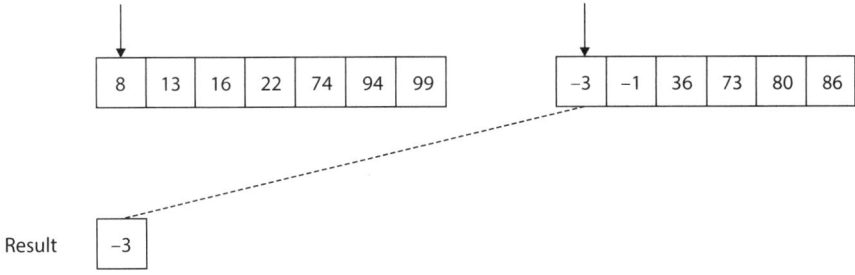

Figure 5.6 Compare the first element of each list and add the smaller one to the result list.

Repeat this step until you've reached the end of both lists.

Challenge: Given the description above, can you write a function merge(*list1*, *list2*) in Python? (Hint: It is a fruitful function)

MERGE SORT ALGORITHM

Now that you've understood the intuition behind the merge algorithm, you can use it for sorting. The idea behind Merge Sort is to first split the unsorted list into lists containing only one element (Figure. 5.7)

Then, we'll progressively recombine neighbouring sorted lists using the merge function we defined earlier (Figure. 5.8)

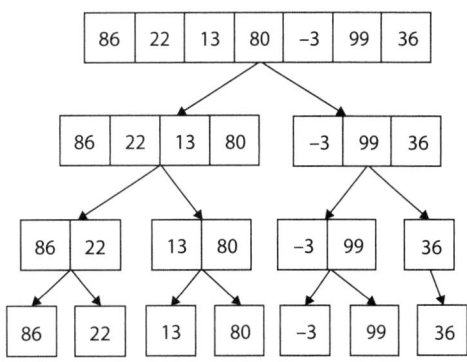

Figure 5.7 First, split the unsorted list progressively until you obtain lists each containing one element.

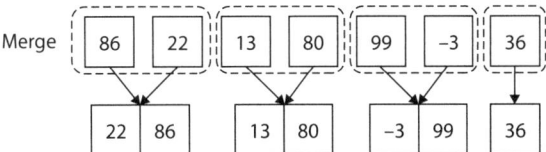

Figure 5.8 Merge by choosing the smaller number from each source list.

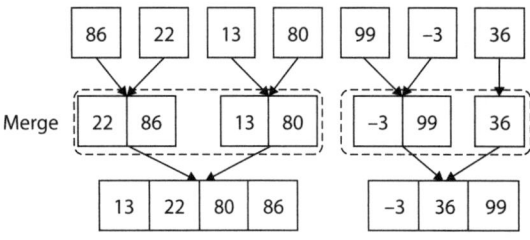

Figure 5.9 Continue merging by choosing the smaller number from each source list.

We continue merging neighbouring lists (Figure. 5.9) until we have merged all of them back into a single list. Can you complete the last step in the Merge Sort algorithm using the diagram above?

While we are not going to focus on the implementation of this algorithm, it is useful to understand Merge Sort and know that there are multiple ways to approach the same problem (here, sorting!)

5.2.4   Review Questions

Time to test how much you understand the content in this chapter. It's totally OK to go back and review!

THEORY AND UNDERSTANDING

- What are the names of the sorting algorithms we learned in this section?
- Do we need to use comparison operators when sorting?
- Which of the two sorting algorithms would you choose if you had a very large amount of data to sort?
- Since sorting takes time, in what practical case would you want to perform sorting to increase the speed of search?

SYNTAX SELF-CHECK

- `myList[0],myList[1] = myList[1],myList[0]`

```
1   a="1"
2   b="2"
3   # swapping
4   temp=a
5   a=b
6   b=temp
```

5.2.5   Practice Exercises

CODING

Now it's time for you to practice by writing some code. When you are done, you can go to the Solutions section on our companion website to compare your answers with ours. Note that there can be many answers to the same question, so don't worry if yours are not the same as ours. The important things are that they produce the same results, and you are able to tell where the differences are and why both answers work.

A MODIFIED SELECTION SORT

In this section, we learned the Selection Sort algorithm, which swapped the minimum number in a list with the first item in the unsorted list. Selection Sort can also be implemented by finding the maximum number in the list, and swapping it with the last item in the unsorted list. Using this updated algorithm, suppose you have the following list of numbers to sort: [11, 7, 12, 14, 19, 1, 6, 18, 8, 20]. Which list represents the partially sorted list after three complete passes of selection sort?

(A)   [7, 11, 12, 1, 6, 14, 8, 18, 19, 20],
(B)   [7, 11, 12, 14, 19, 1, 6, 18, 8, 20],
(C)   [11, 7, 12, 14, 1, 6, 8, 18, 19, 20],
(D)   [11, 7, 12, 14, 8, 1, 6, 18, 19, 20]

Write this version of Selection Sort as a function.

CODING THE MERGE FUNCTION

Define a function that receives as input parameters two sorted lists, and returns a third list which is the merge of both lists. This is the function that is used as part of the Merge Sort algorithm. Note that the lengths of the two input lists may be different. Test it for at least three different cases.

5.3   MAP, FILTER, REDUCE

Searching and sorting are classic conceptual problems in computer science to process lists of items. In addition to **search** and **sort**, especially since the advent of the Internet, new common patterns of list processing have been identified.

Map, **filter**, and **reduce** are common patterns that you may encounter in your daily life while using applications on the Internet.

Map: Apply a particular function to every element in the list. For example, in a list of products you are buying from an online store, you may wish to apply a 50% discount on each item.

Filter: Filter out certain parts of a list based on a condition. For example, in a list of T-shirts on a store website, you may wish to filter on only those less than $10.

Reduce: Reduce the list contents into one value. For example, in a list of prices of items in your shopping cart, you may wish to find the total price.

A FUNCTIONAL PROGRAMMING PARADIGM

Python is what is called a procedural or imperative programming language. This means that the program is executed from top to bottom in a step-by-step, command-like fashion. But there are other styles of programming languages:

- Functional programming: All things in a program are functions (e.g., LISP, Scheme, OCaml)
- Logic programming: All things in a program are predicates (rules and facts) (e.g., Prolog)
- Object-oriented programming: All things in a program are objects (states and methods) (e.g., Java, C++)

In order to perform the above **map**, **filter**, and **reduce** operations, one straightforward method in Python is to use an iterative approach, which is a common pattern in **procedural** programming. Specifically, you could use a loop to solve these problems on lists.

An alternative method is to use a **functional programming** approach. While we will not go into the details of functional programming here, one hallmark of functional programming is that you can use functions in a similar way as you currently use variables. For instance, you can pass a function as an argument to another function.

Map, **filter**, and **reduce** lend themselves well to the functional programming approach. Here are some code examples to see how this would work.

MAP

Let's say we want to apply a 50% discount to a list of product prices. In other words, we want to apply a function, let's call it `halfPrice`, to a list of prices. The code would look something like this, where we first define the `halfPrice` function to return a modified price, then use `map` to apply that function to the list `productPrices`.

```
1  # Map Example
2  def halfPrice(price):
3      return 0.5*price
4
5  productPrices = [12,5,17,8,5]
6  discountedPrices = map(halfPrice,productPrices)
7  print(list(discountedPrices))
```

The code example above will print out [6.0, 2.5, 8.5, 4.0, 2.5]. In it, we have defined a helper function `halfPrice`, which defines how one item should be modified. Then, we have applied that function to the list `productPrices` by using the built-in `map` function in Python. This `map` function is a special kind of function called a **higher-order function**, which takes another function as an argument. Note that `map` returns a map object, which must be converted back to a list using the `list` function in order to proceed with processing, including printing.

FILTER

Filter is another higher-order built-in function in Python, and works in a similar way. Imagine that `filter` is like a sieve that only lets through prices in the list that are less than ten dollars. We will create a helper function `lowPrice` that returns a Boolean value `True` if the price is less than 10. Then, as with map, we provide filter with two arguments: the function `lowPrice` and a list of prices to filter.

```
1  # Filter Example
2  def lowPrice(price):
3      return price < 10
4
5  productPrices = [12,5,17,8,5]
6  lowCostPrices = filter(lowPrice,productPrices)
7
8  print(list(lowCostPrices))
```

This will print out [5, 8, 5]. Now, we have provided examples here that work on lists of numbers, but map, filter, and reduce also work on other kinds of data, like *strings*. For instance, if we had a list of T-shirt slogans, and only want to filter out those sayings that were short and sweet, and specifically less than 12 characters long:

```
1   # Filter Example
2   def shortPhrase(phrase):
3       return len(phrase) < 12
4
5   slogans = ["Surf's Up!",
6              "Happy Camper", "Have a Nice Day"]
7   shortSlogans = filter(shortPhrase,slogans)
8
9   print(list(shortSlogans))
```

This would print **["Surf's Up!"]**.

REDUCE

Finally, let's see an example of reduce. In our price list example, reduce could be used to reduce the list contents into one value, like the total cost of all the prices in the list. It might help to think of reduce in terms of reducing a soup into something more concentrated.

To perform a reduce, you need to define a helper function, just as with map and filter. But this time, your helper function needs to take two arguments. The goal of this function is to define how you should combine two elements. Let's try with our example of calculating the sum total of a list of integers. How would you do it for the case of two integers?

```
1   # Reduce Helper Function
2   def sumTotal(price1,price2):
3       return price1 + price2
```

Next, you will need to import the reduce function from the functools package. Then, as before, apply the reduce function using your helper function and the list.

```
1   # Reduce Example - Total Price
2   from functools import reduce
3
4   def sumTotal(price1,price2):
5       return price1 + price2
6
7   productPrices = [12,5,17,8,5]
8   totalPrice = reduce(sumTotal,productPrices)
9   print(totalPrice)
```

This should print 47. Internally, reduce applies the function recursively. In other words, reduce continually applies the function sumTotal(price1,price2) to the list. First, sumTotal is applied to the first two elements in the sequence, then sumTotal is applied to the result and the third element, and so on, until only one element is left.

Here is another example involving strings. Let's imagine that you want to combine the names of all your friends into a single string separated by stars.

```
1   # Reduce Example - Combine Initials
2   from functools import reduce
3
4   def combine(name1,name2):
5       return name1 + "*" + name2
6
7   names = ["Bonnie","Emily","Angel","Nicole"]
8   print(reduce(combine,names))
```

This will print out Bonnie*Emily*Angel*Nicole. To understand a bit more about how this works, note that the following code would *not* print out the initials BEAN. What will it print out? Try it!

```
1   # Reduce Example - Combine Initials
2   from functools import reduce
3
4   def combine(name1,name2):
5       return name1[0] + name2[0]
6
7   names = ["Bonnie","Emily","Angel","Nicole"]
8   print(reduce(combine,names))
```

5.3.1   Learning Outcomes

At the end of this unit, you will be able to ...

MAP/FILTER/REDUCE

- understand the general patterns of map, filter, and reduce
- give example applications of map, filter, and reduce
- convert iterative list operations into code using map, filter, and reduce when applicable
- write functions that can be passed as augments to map, filter, and reduce, given a program description

5.3.2   Review Questions

Time to test how much you understand the content in this chapter. It's totally OK to go back and review!

THEORY AND UNDERSTANDING

- What do map, filter, and reduce have in common?
- What are examples of when you would you use each of map, filter, or reduce?
- Can a function be passed in as a parameter to another function?
- Out of map, filter, and reduce, which will return a list?
- Of map, filter, and reduce, which one requires the import of functools (i.e., is not a built-in Python function)?

SYNTAX SELF-CHECK

```
1   def mymapfunc(x):
2     # return a modified x
3
4   def myfilterfunc(x):
5     # return True/False
6     # given a condition on x
7
8   from functools import reduce
9   def myreducefunc(x,y):
10    # return a single value given x and y
```

- `map(mymapfunc,myList)`
- `filter(myfilterfunc,myList)`
- `reduce(myfunc,myList)`

5.3.3   Practice Exercises

CODING PRACTICE

Write a program that asks the user to type a sequence of integers (separated by commas) and then prints them back to the display as a list, except that only those that are greater than 5 are included. Assume the user types as asked. Provide two versions to solve this problem:

- using a `for`- or `while`-loop
- using `map`/`filter`/`reduce`

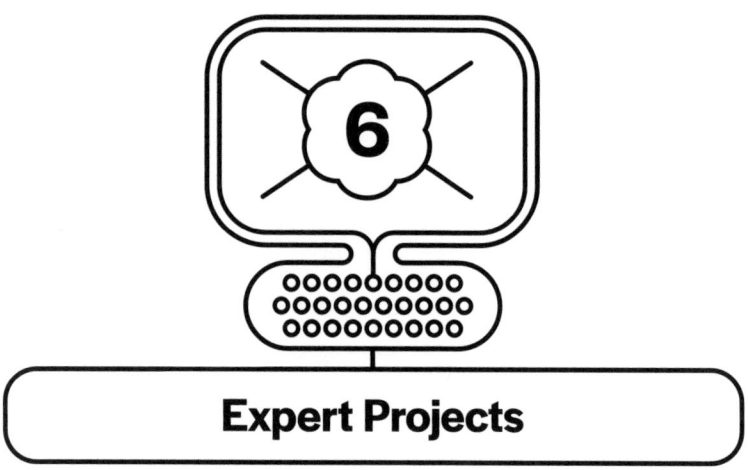

6

Expert Projects

Challenge yourself with projects that put your understanding of all the materials to test! Here you'll find projects that you can implement yourself to synthesize your knowledge from this book.

6.1   AUDIO-VISUAL LANGUAGE LEARNING CHATBOT

In this project, you will develop an interactive text-, image- and audio-based language learning app for people to learn an endangered Indigenous language. The language is called Blackfoot, and is spoken by Indigenous nations in Alberta, Canada and Montana, USA. There is currently little interactive software available for people to learn the language, and so you are going to create it!

TOPICS

This project will allow you to practice the following concepts:

- Creating an interactive text-based chatbot
- Displaying an image to the screen
- Creating, reading and working with data from text files
- Using the dictionary data type
- Creating and using your own custom functions
- Playing and manipulating audio files
- Creating custom graphics for your application

This project was created in collaboration with Dr. Eldon Yellowhorn.

APPLICATION DEMONSTRATION

The language learning chatbot lets the learner visit various locations around town (e.g., town, restaurant) and learn the vocabulary relating to each of these locations (e.g., cinema, cafe). Your chatbot will offer to teach them words, as well as test them on what they have learned. Importantly, your chatbot will not only display the words but will allow the learner to hear the words through their speakers or headphones. You can find below a video depicting the basic application flow of what you will build.

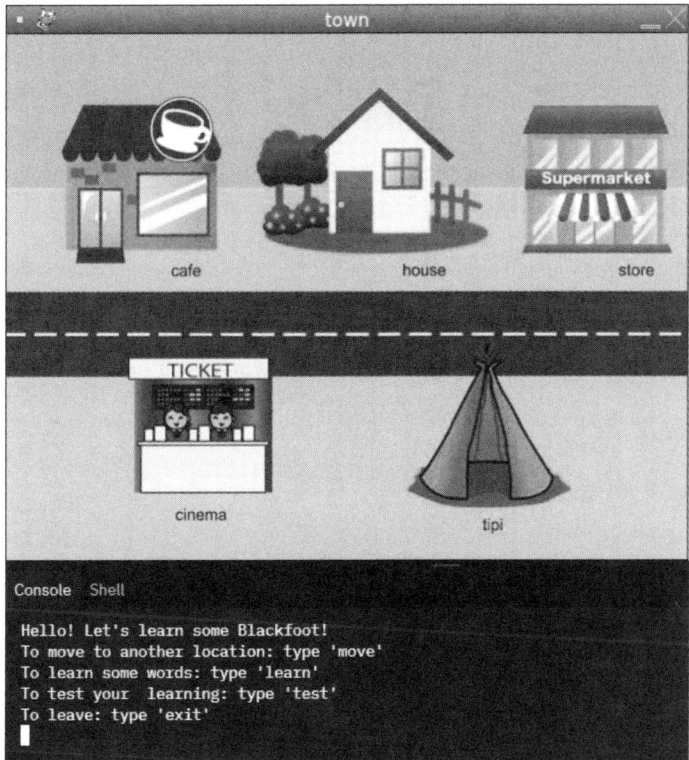

Figure 6.1 In this project, you'll create a chatbot that lets you navigate around a town to learn vocabulary in Blackfoot.

You can find a demonstration video here: https://www.youtube.com/watch?v=_ndQlNPBixw.

YOUR TASK

For this project, you will be combining the concepts learned from the practice exercises to make an interactive chatbot that uses audio and imagery to help users learn Blackfoot.

BASIC CHATBOT FEATURES

Here are the basic features you should implement in this project. The user should be able to stay in the program until they type "exit."

1. **Move.** The user should be able to move between the two locations provided (town and restaurant) and the image displayed should change accordingly.
2. **Learn and Test.** For each location include:
   - a "Learn" function: When the user types in an English word, the chatbot responds with the Blackfoot translation.
   - a "Test" function: The chatbot asks the user for the English translation of 10 random Blackfoot words.

3. **Audio.** The corresponding Blackfoot audio should play whenever Blackfoot vocabulary is shown.
4. **Translation data.** Blackfoot-English translation data should be stored in one or more dictionaries.

See the video for more details on what the chatbot might say for each feature.

ADVANCED CHATBOT FEATURES

- **Custom functions.** Organize your code in modules and custom functions.
- **File storage.** Place the Blackfoot-English translations into a .csv file and load them into a dictionary instead of hard-coding the data into your program.
- **Five scenes.** Create custom graphics and include three other locations. See below for tips.
- **Speech synthesis.** Include a "speech synthesis" function that allows the user to construct their own phrases in Blackfoot. See the Blackfoot Project Vocabulary section for example sentences, as well as the concat function under Tips, below, for more details.

TIPS

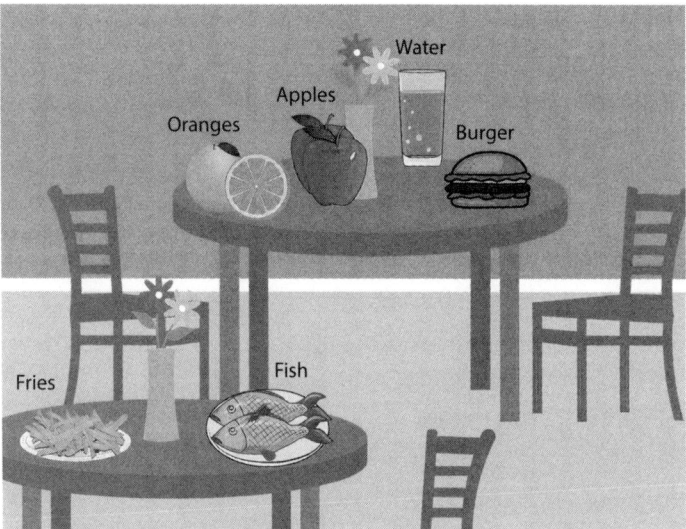

Figure 6.2 An example image for the restaurant scene. Use it or create your own!

One way to create custom graphics is to:

- Find images (ones with transparent backgrounds work a bit better; they are typically in .png format) using Google Image Search.
- Note: Images found may be subject to copyright.

  – Go to "Tools", then select "Creative Commons licenses" from the "Usage Rights" filter.
  – When you click on filtered images, they will have licensing information. Click on "License details" to check, and follow the terms of use before using the images you have found.

- Put the .png images together in software such as Google Slides.
- Download the slide as a .jpg or .png, and resize in a program such as Paint if necessary.

You will also need the csimage.py file from Chapter 4: Image Magic to display your images to the screen for this project.

AUDIO

In order to develop the Audio portion of this project, download the necessary .wav files from http://blackfoot-revitalization.cs.sfu.ca/TeachingResources.

To play audio for the "speech synthesis" component, the following concat function has been provided. You will need to import the wave module for the concat function to work properly.

```
1   def concat(infiles,outfile):
2       """
3       Input:
4       - infiles: list of .wav files to concatenate,
5         e.g. ["hello.wav","there.wav"]
6       - outfile: name of concatenated output .wav file
7         e.g. "hellothere.wav"
8       Returns: None
9       """
10      data= []
11      for infile in infiles:
12          w = wave.open(infile, 'rb')
13          data.append( \
14          [w.getparams(), w.readframes(w.getnframes())] )
15          w.close()
16      output = wave.open(outfile, 'wb')
17      output.setparams(data[0][0])
18      for i in range(len(data)):
19          output.writeframes(data[i][1])
20      output.close()
```

BLACKFOOT PROJECT VOCABULARY

Use the Blackfoot vocabulary below to create your translation and/or support files for your project. There are a total of five different locations.

1. Town

   - aisaksittoo - cinema
   - itaohpomoapii - store
   - itaisimmioapii - night club
   - itoiyo'pii - cafe
   - naapoiyiss - house
   - niitoiyiss - tipi

2. Restaurant

- aohkii - water
- mamii - fish
- aotahkoinamm - orange
- apaisstaaminattsi - apple
- paataakistsi - potatoes/fries
- pikkiaaksin - burger
- pisatsoyiikan - dessert
- napayin - bread
- siksikimmii - tea
- iitapsiksikimmii - coffee

3. Home

- makapoiyiss - bathroom
- itoiyo'soap - kitchen
- aiksistomatomahka - car
- kitsim - door
- aisspaohpii - elevator
- ksisstsikomstan - window
- imitaa - dog

4. Family

- ninaa - man
- aakii - woman
- aakiikoan - girl
- saahkomaapi - boy
- iksisst - mother
- inn - father

5. Greetings

- oki - hello
- oki napi - hello friend
- tsa niita'piiwa? - how are you?
- tsikohssokopii. kistoo? - I'm doing good, you?
- matohkwiikii - not too bad
- okí - let's go
- aa - yes
- saa - no

VOCABULARY FOR SPEECH SYNTHESIS

The following are example sentences that should be generated for the speech synthesis component. Examine the pattern of the Blackfoot sentences to devise a way for your program to generate grammatically and semantically correct sentences in Blackfoot.

1. Example sentences

- Aapinakos nitaakitapoo aisaksittoo - Tomorrow I will go to the cinema
- Ksisskanaotonni nitaaksoyi napayin - This morning I will eat bread
- Annohk nitaakitapoo itoiyo'pii - Today I will go to the cafe

2. Time words

    - annohk - today
    - ksisskanaotonni - this morning
    - aapinakos - tomorrow

3. Verbs

    - nitaakitapoo - I will go
    - nitaaksoyi - I will eat

6.2   INTERACTIVE IMAGE PROCESSOR

Have you ever used any image processing software like Adobe Photoshop, GIMP, or Corel-DRAW to modify an image? Perhaps you applied a filter, or simply rotated the image? In this project, you are going to create your own image processing software. Plus, you will add a computer vision feature to "detect" an object in your photo.

Figure 6.3 In this project, you will create image filters! Here is an example of applying a flip-horizontal filter.

TOPICS

This project will allow you to practice the following concepts:

- Creating an interactive text-based chatbot
- Using `while`-loops to obtain user input
- Creating and using custom functions
- Writing nested `for`-loops to access pixels of images
- Performing manipulations on 2D arrays
- Processing colours for a computer vision task

YOUR TASK

For this project, you will be combining the concepts learned from the practice exercises to make an interactive chatbot that takes an image and modifies it according to the features below.

BASIC FEATURES

Here are the basic features to implement in this project.

1. Horizontal flip. Flip the image horizontally (like a mirror).
2. Warm filter. Gives the image a warm tone. The warm colour of a pixel is calculated by scaling the original R value up and B value down using this formula:

- Scale up: If the value is less than 64, the scaled-up value is value/64 * 80; if the value is 64 or above but less than 128, the scaled-up value is (value–64)/(128–64) * (160–80) + 80; otherwise, the scaled-up value is (value–128)/(255–128) * (255–160) + 160
- Scale down: if the value is less than 64, the scaled-down value is value/64 * 50; if the value is 64 or above but less than 128, the scaled-down value is (value-64)/(128–64) * (100–50) + 50; otherwise, the scaled-up value is (value–128)/(255–128) * (255–100) + 100. For example, if a pixel has [100, 255, 200] as its RGB colour, the warm colour of this pixel will be [125, 255, 187], where the R value is scaled up and the B value is scaled down. Note that the scaling might result in a float number, so you need to convert it into an integer. To make things easier, consider first defining a function that does the scale up calculation and a function that does the scale down calculation.

ADVANCED FEATURES

Before

After

 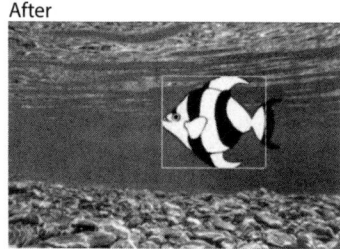

Figure 6.4 Write a function to draw a box around the yellow fish in this photo (see companion website to view the original fish colour in yellow).

1. Rotate right. Rotates the image right by 90 degrees. This operation requires creating a new image with width equal to the original height and height equal to the original width. (Hint: Use the nested for-loop structure to copy a row of pixels into a column of pixels).
2. Zoom. Double both width and height (so the size is actually four times as before). This operation requires creating a new image with width equal to two times the original width and height equal to two times the original height. To "build" a bigger image, each pixel from the original image becomes a 2x2 block of pixels in the result image. For example, the pixels at result[0][0], result[0][1], result[1][0], and result[1][1] will have the same RGB values of the pixel at original[0][0].
3. Locate fish. The cat in your photo is hungry! Using the provided fish.jpg, detect the yellow colour of the fish and draw a green (0, 255, 0) bounding box around the fish. The line should be one pixel wide and surround the yellow areas of the fish. You may import the copy module and use its deepcopy() function for this operation. See below for more tips.

INTERACTIVE IMAGE PROCESSOR

The program should provide a chatbot-like interface to fulfil the following:

- Take user input (0/1/2/3/4/5) using a while-loop to determine which of the five manipulation options described above (1/2/3/4/5) they want to apply.
- If the user enters 0, exit.

- If the user enters 1/2/3/4/5, perform the manipulation, then save the resulting image as a new image under the name `result-optionX.jpg`, where X is the user input option; for example, `result-option1.jpg` should contain the image flipped horizontally. Once the manipulation and saving is done, ask the user for an input again.
- If the user enters something other than the expected input (e.g., 12), display the message `Sorry, I don't understand 12` and take the user input again.
- Each manipulation should be done starting with the original image; i.e., the manipulations are not applied to the resulting image from a previous manipulation.
- Define **one function** for each manipulation option.

TIPS

To detect the yellow colour, you can use the code provided below, which returns a list containing three values, for Hue, Saturation, and Value (brightness) given an RGB color. You may refer to an HSV colour picker online to help you define a good range for hue, saturation, and value to detect the fish. The HSV representation is often used for graphics software because it is slightly closer to how humans perceive colour. It can be a better representation for this computer vision task, because an object with a particular hue might have a different brightness, depending on the amount of light hitting it at a particular time.

```
1
2  def rgb_to_hsv(r, g, b):
3      """
4      Input: values of a pixel in RGB colour space
5      Output: values in HSV colour space
6      From
7      https://www.w3resource.com/python-exercises/math/
8      python-math-exercise-77.php
9      """
10     r, g, b = r/255.0, g/255.0, b/255.0
11     mx = max(r, g, b)
12     mn = min(r, g, b)
13     df = mx-mn
14     if mx == mn:
15         h = 0
16     elif mx == r:
17         h = (60 * ((g-b)/df) + 360) % 360
18     elif mx == g:
19         h = (60 * ((b-r)/df) + 120) % 360
20     elif mx == b:
21         h = (60 * ((r-g)/df) + 240) % 360
22     if mx == 0:
23         s = 0
24     else:
25         s = (df/mx)*100
26     v = mx*100
27     return [h, s, v]
```

Debugging hints: (1) You can set the fish's yellow pixels to a different color to understand what your algorithm has detected. (2) You can try to create a function to draw a green box in a specified location, and with a specified width and height. This will help you understand if your drawing function works, independently of the fish detection. Note: This feature only needs to work for the provided image's fish and background. However, you may not hard-code the values of the box (e.g., location, width, height); they must be calculated by inspecting the image (your program should work if the fish is in a different location in the image!)

EXTENSIONS

If you've completed the above, try some other ways to extend your project! For example, provide an option for the user to enter the name of the photo to open. Or, investigate other filters, such as grayscale or sepia, by searching for formulas on the Internet. Finally, you can try to make your program "additive"; that is, it should apply filters one on top of the other, instead of directly on the original image.

FILES AND RESOURCES

A starter kit of assets, including photos to modify and use in your program, have been provided on this book's companion website.

You will also need the `csimage.py` file from Section 4.2.3: Image Magic to read and load your images.

Index

Pages in italics indicate figures

accumulator patterns: initialization and, 46, 66; maximum value and, 68; recommendation systems and, xii, 45–46, 58, 66, 68, 70–71

algorithms: chatbots and, 11–12, 18; computer science and, x, 1–8; concept of, 1–2; drawing trees and, 102; English, xiii; image processing and, 138; as instructions, 1; interactive drawings and, 72; Linear Search, 112–17; many locations and, 112, 117; Merge Sort, 112, 118, 122–25; Palindrome Checker, 112, 118; recommendation systems and, 45; recursive, 102; search, 112–17, 122; Selection Sort, 112, 118–25; swapping, 112, 119; as way of thinking, 1

Analytical Engine, 3

arrays, 73, 91–92, 135

assignment, 28, 47, 57

audio, 130–35

Babbage, Charles, 3

Basic Recursive Tree, 106–8

binary search, 112–17, 122

Blackfoot Project Vocabulary, 130–34

blocks, 4, 30

Boolean expressions: chatbots and, 9, 11, 21–22, 29; image processing and, 88, 100; interactive drawings and, 75–76; keep_looping, 75–76; learning outcomes and, 11; logical operators and, 21–22; map, filter, reduce operations and, 126; searching and, 113–14; True/False, 11, 21, 26, 76, 88–90, 93–97, 113–18, 129

brackets, 16

Bubble Tea Menu Bot, 36–38

C++ language, 2, 8, 125

capitalize() function, 53

casting, 57

chaining: chatbots and, 10, 34, 42, 44; method, 34, 63, 67; recommendation systems and, 63, 67

chatbots: advanced programming and, x–xi; algorithms and, 11–12, 18; Amazon and, 9; Blackfoot Project Vocabulary, 130–34; Boolean expressions and, 9, 11, 21–22, 29;

Bubble Tea Menu Bot, 36–38; Canadian measurement, 34–36; chaining, 10, 34, 42, 44; Chip Rater, 45, 50–51; coding and, 29, 42–43, 132; Coffee Bot, 27–28; comments and, 11–13, 18, 22; Common Interests Finder, 45, 65–66, 70; concatenation and, 9, 11, 13, 26, 29, 133; conditionals and, 9, 11, 18–22, 29, 34–35, 42; Cookie Drawer, 72, 76–79; CSV files, 132; data types and, 11, 13, 16, 130; dictionaries and, 130, 132; error and, 9, 25, 30–31, 44; Favourite Pets Finder, 45, 59–65; Food, 9, 32–34; for-loops and, 10, 29, 37–44; format and, 132; Fortune Cookie, 9, 27; functions and, 10–17, 25–31, 34, 40–44, 130–35; Green Screen Magic Bot, 72, 91–96; Greetings, 9, 12–18; headers and, 11–12, 18, 29; Horoscope, 9, 22–26, 32; How's It Going Bot, 18–22, 31–32; import and, 11, 15–18, 26, 28, 133; in keyword and, 10, 20, 25, 29, 31–32, 53; Input Validator, 72, 76, 82; integers and, 10, 29, 42; interactivity and, 9–10, 13, 15, 18, 29–30, 72–81, 130–31; interpreters and, 28, 30; keywords and, 10, 19–21, 25–32, 36, 42; language and, 9, 28, 31, 130–35; learning outcomes and, 11; lists and, 9–10, 15–18, 25, 39, 42; logical operators and, 21–22; with loops, 29–30; lower() function and, 29, 31–35, 39–42, 44; mathematics and, 28, 137; Mindreader Game, 9, 38–42; modules and, 9, 11, 17, 26, 28, 132–33; Movie Rater, 45, 52–54, 59; New Year's Bot, 9, 43–44; Number Guessing Game, 72, 112, 116; operators and, 11, 17, 21–22, 26, 28, 31, 44; with personality, 10–28; Popular Cafe Finder, 45–50, 52, 54, 59, 66; popularity of, ix; programming and, x–xi, 9, 16, 28–31, 35, 37, 44; randomness and, 9, 11, 15–18, 26–28, 31, 40–41, 131; relational operators and, 11, 21–22; repetition and, 37, 40, 42; robustness and, 29–33, 43–44; Similar People Finder, 45, 65–66, 70; speech synthesis and, 132–35; Star Wars, 9, 65; strings and, 11, 17, 29, 31, 42; syntax and, 26, 30, 42; True/False